FREEMASONRY
in
the Aquarian Age

A Vision

FREEMASONRY
in
the Aquarian Age

A vision

Else Marie Post

© 2012 Else Marie Post
Translated by Annette Trap Friis
First published in Danish 2009: *Frimureri i Vandbærerens Tidsalder*
Composition, illustrations and cover: Jens Rasmussen
Publishing: Books om Demand GmbH, Copenhagen, Denmark
Print: Books on Demand GmbH, Norderstedt, Germany
ISBN: 9788771144390

Contents

Introduction

Just like the origin of freemasonry fades away in distant ages and in distant and invisible horizons, the purpose of freemasonry and its work through times faded away and was blurred.

Freemasonry has moved further and further away from its original beauty and purpose; it has been exposed to distortion and to some extent of crystallization and has thereby ended up in a stagnated and sectarian form where importance has been given to the sense of the outer form – and not to the inner spiritual significance. Importance has been given to symbols and allegories and great focus was put to the Grand Master and not to the work on the floor. The lodge was not been seen as an integrated whole.

Simultaneously with this gloomy description freemasonry *has* preserved and protected the core of the ageless wisdom; freemasonry has preserved mystery-rituals with facts, details and the structure intact.

Time has now come to restore freemasonry to its true purpose. This implies that a change in attitudes and views must take place so that the work will be focused on the inner spiritual *significance* of the mysteries. In that way the power and the efficiency in the work of the lodge will be provided and the true meaning of the work and the use of the *word* which lies in the regularity of the rituals and the sanctified formality of the ordinated ceremonies will appear clearly.

In the coming age, the Aquarian age, freemasonry will achieve a crucial role, i.e. if it is capable to cleans itself of the crystallization of the Piscean age. The Aquarian age is widely influenced by the seventh ray under which freemasonry also functions. Freemasonry can take part in preparing the way for the Kingdom of God to come to Earth and for the Masters of the Hierarchy to come and walk among us humans just as they did in former times in Atlantis. Freemasonry will experience receiving hierachal help to restore the ancient mysteries – when significant changes have been taken and when man has comprehended the spirit of freemasonry instead of taken it literally.

When this has happened :
- freemasonry will work together with the world of significance
- freemasons will cooperate with God and the inner divine worlds by fastening on and conceiving the Plan and working to encourage realization of the Plan in the world
- the freemason-lodge will become a true place of inflow from divine light, love and power
- freemasonry will educate and form human beings to become true servers and channels of inflow of will, love and light of the Kingdom of God
- the freemason will be a true server

In coming time the initiation-mysteries will be revealed og will prepare the coming of the Kingdom of God.

In the same way as churches have lost their inner life, freemasonry has lost the true reality which it once had, but in its forms and rituals truth is kept and can be restored. The true mysteries can emerge again, and the real source of revelation can be revealed.

Freemasonry, esoteric groups and certain churches working to promote the Plan on Earth – not only in a symbolic sense, but in factual sense – can be the centres on the mundane and fysical level through which the Inner World Government send help to Earth and mankind.

To be of use for the inner levels, i.e. the Hierarchy and Shamballa, it is necessary to change the focus in the work, and it is necessary to cleans freemasonry from old distorted opinions and understandings, cleans ingrained bad habits which belong to the world of the personality. Instead they must work persistingly to build up the Anthakarana, so that a real and conscious coorporation with Masters and the Hierachy can take place. In that way the freemason-lodge can help the Kingdom of God to manifest on Earth, and the freemason can become a server in the true meaning of the word.[1]

Does freemasonry wish to work with the *real* world? Do freemasons wish to coorporate with the inner world – not only *symbolically* but *in actual fact*? Do freemasons wish to change focus from the world of the *personality* to the world of the *soul* and the *spirit* – not only *symbolically* but *in actual fact*? Do freemasons wish to coorporate consciously with and in the energies and influences which are flowing to us from the inner worlds? Do freemasons wish to be active partners in the process that is taking place and which will continue for the next two thousand years? Is freemasonry able to cleans itself and change attitudes and focus? Will freemasons be able to break down old and worn-out habits? Will freemasonry be able to restore a new system of education which can help seekers to develop spiritually – not only *symbolically* but *in actual fact*?

This book is based on a vision of freemasonry in the Aquarian age which the author received at an inspiration some years ago. At that time she for some years in her inner work had tried to grasp and understand the inner essence of freemasonry.

In the vision the freemason-lodge in the future looked so purified, so radiant and shining and most of all so powerful that words cannot describe it. Sisters and Brothers in the Lodge were living shining columns, and the four columns – yes there were four columns one in each corner of the world – they radiated with such a brightness that it cannot be described in words.

Truely it was a temple which connected Heaven and Earth – and the connection were human beings, purified and transparent! The inner God-men radiated; they truely had surrendered to the inner work! And in the column in North radiated – it was the Master of the freemasonry himself, the Master Rakocy, also called the Comte de St. Germain, he had taken his place!

How beautiful! How fantastic! How wonderful!

For a long time after the vison the author continued working with 'Freemasonry in the Future'. The vision she saw and the things she experienced were completely different from what she saw at meetings in the lodge.

Why was that? How was it to be understood? The questions that came up were countless.

Attempting to conceive the vision of freemasonry in the future in the Aquarian age she continued her meditative quest over the following period: "What would freemasonry make able to bring this vision into realization?" Out of this inspirations and understandings came, and the following studies resulted in this present book.

Through these studies the author later discovered that in fact there were references that predicted some of the same things which she had experienced in the vision. And it was in the course of that proces that she realized that in fact it had been the light of the Master she had seen in North.

The text is provided with many notes so that the interested student can become absorbed in the source and the context from where quotations and understandings are taken.

Where does Freemasonry come from?

Since time began freemasonry was established and organized under a direct influence from Sirius. It was formed – as far as it was possible – with certain Sirius-institutions as the ideal and also with a slight ressemblance to our planetary life – seen in the light of the eternal now. Its "Blue Lodge" with the three degrees are related to the three big groups of life on Sirius because nature-realms as we know them do not exist. These groups receive all those who choose the fourth way and train them in the way to exist and in the type of life that exist on Sirius. From our point of view the least developed Sirius-lives are all initiates of very high degree. Therefore freemasonry is connected to the path of development to Sirius in a very special way. Through time the traditions of freemasons have been kept, the terminology has changed from time to time, its word of power has been re-interpreted and consequently freemasonry has moved further and further away from its original beauty and purpose.[2]

To understand the influences on the life-proces and development on Earth and in us humans a short description of the cosmic coherence and a survey in chart follows.

Deep in the universe there are three big centres, the Great Bear, Sirius and the Pleiades. These centres send out their energies with the rays via the zodiac signs, further on to Solar-Logos and further again through the planets and thereby influence development on Earth.

The Great Bear is dominated by the energy of the Father which is power-will and transmits energy via Shamballa to Earth.
Sirius is dominated by the energy of the Son which is love-wisdom and flows via the Hierarchy and the Masters to Earth.
The Pleiades is dominated by the energy of the Mother or the Holy Spirit and streams via mankind into the Earth.

The cosmic network of rays

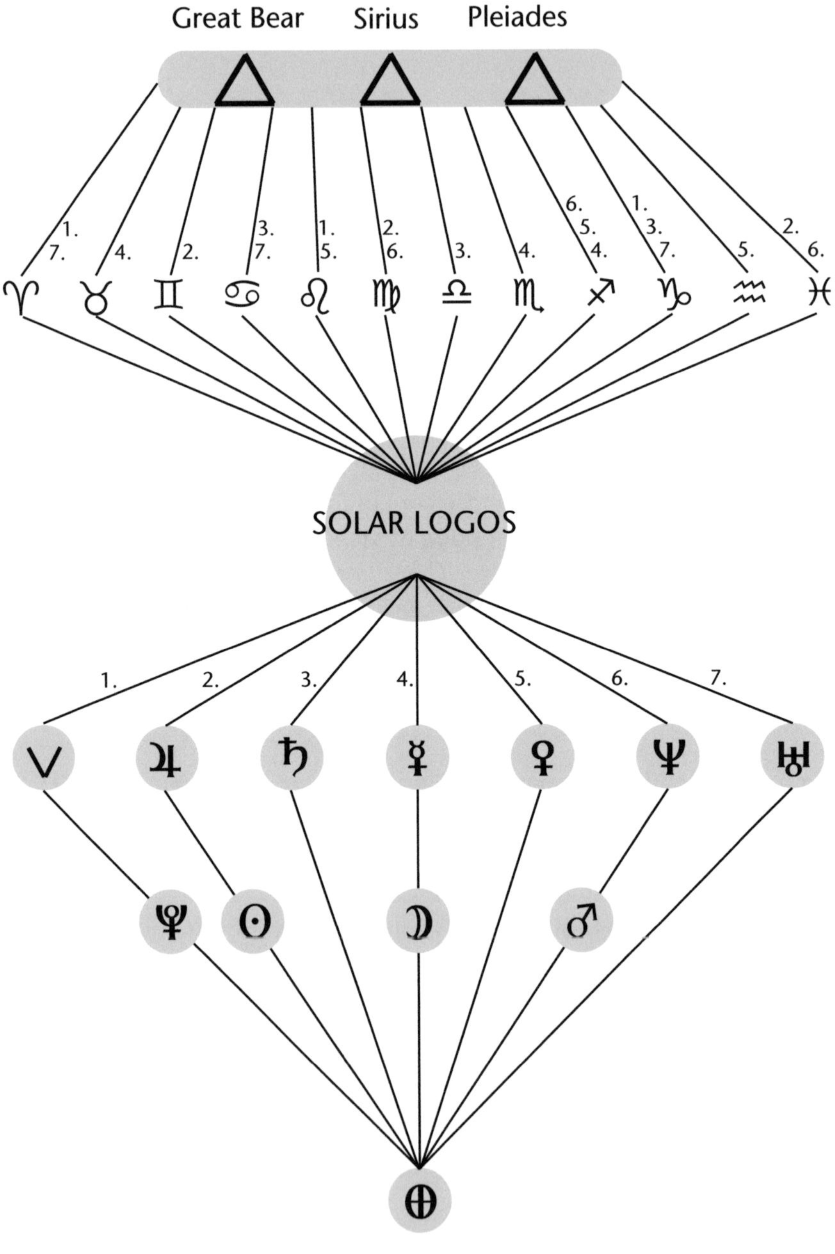
Great Bear
Sirius
Pleiades
SOLAR LOGOS

Chart 1. The cosmic network.[3]

The energy from these centres in the universe are sent with the rays out through the twelve zodiac signs. In chart 1 the signs are to be read from left: Aries transmits the 1st and the 7th ray, Taurus transmits 4th ray, Gemini 2nd ray. In the chart the rays pass through the following signs: Cancer, Leo, Virgo, Libra, Scorpio, Sagittarius, Capricorn, Aquarius and Pisces.

From the zodiac signs the energies are sent through Solar-Logos where they are transformed and sent further through the planets and down to Earth.

Under Solar-Logos there is a row of the seven sacred planets: Vulcan, Jupiter, Saturn, Venus, Neptune and Uranus.
Below are the 4 non-sacred planets: Pluto, the Sun, the Moon and Mars.

The chart shows, how ray 1 is sent through the sacred planet Vulcan and the non-sacred planet Pluto further to Earth. In that way you can see from the illustration which planets transmit which energies.
Earth is a non-sacred planet and belongs among the rest of non-sacred planets, but of graphic reasons it is placed in the buttom of the chart. The survey does not show the secundary influences of the rays, neither the reciprocal connections between the planets.

The Earth makes up a planetsystem which consists of seven planes. The whole development of the Earth is managed by the Inner King of the Earth, Sanat Kumara who resides in Shamballa where the Will and Purpose of God is known. See chart 2 page 14 and chart 4 page 26-27.

From this place decisions and streams are sent via the divine contemplatives to the Hierachy who resides on the Buddhic plane.
The work of the Hierarchy is managed by the World Teacher who at the moment is Christ. The Hierarchy consists of highly developed Masters who are able to grasp the Plan from Shamballa. They work on the seven rays and their work is to inspire and influence human beings to carry out different assignments according to the Plan.

A group of initiates and the new group of Worldservers who through their inner development have constructed the Antahkarana are able to grasp the inspirations of the Masters – fully or partially – and they are mediators to the masses of men.

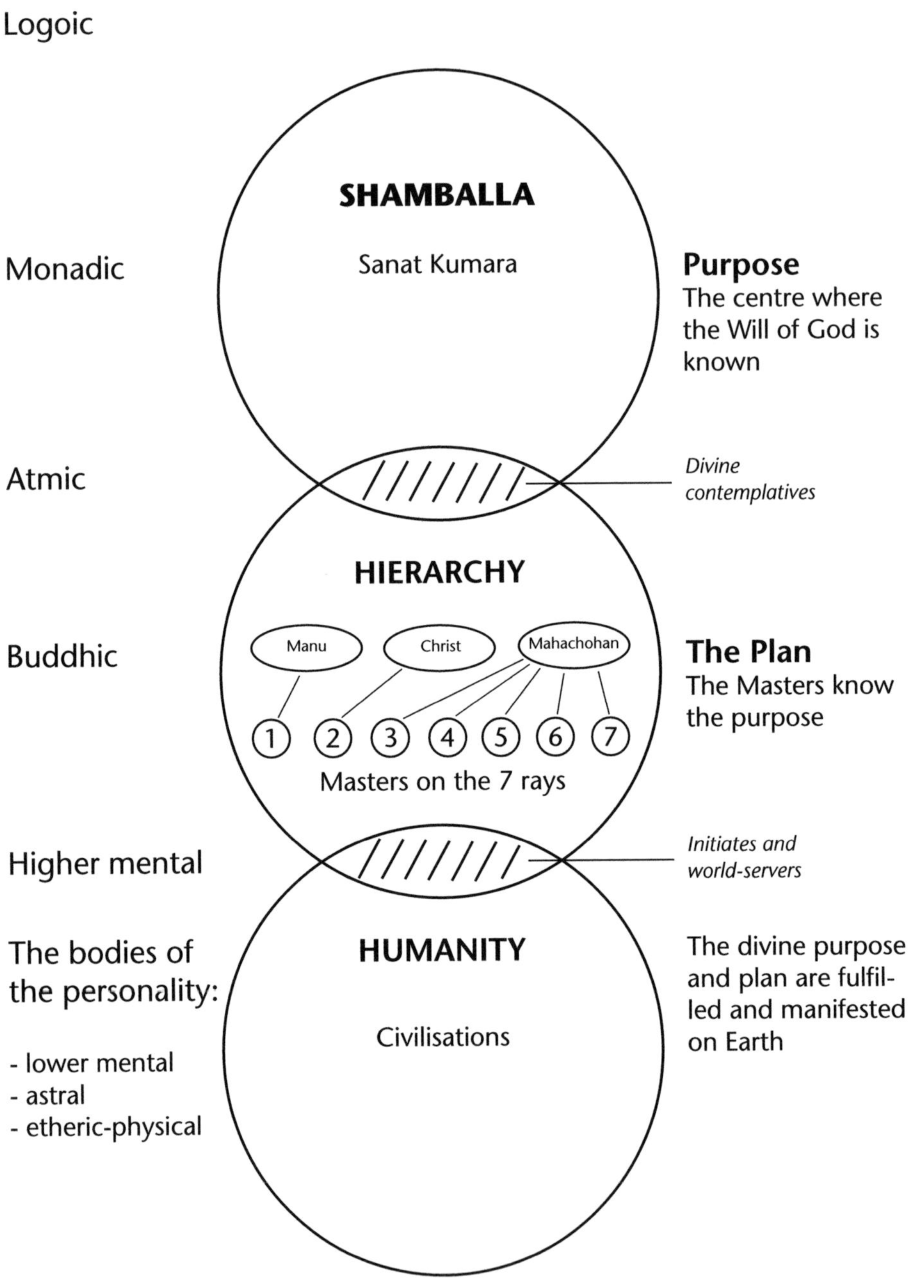

Logoic

SHAMBALLA

Sanat Kumara

Monadic

Purpose
The centre where
the Will of God is
known

Atmic

*Divine
contemplatives*

HIERARCHY

Buddhic

Manu   Christ   Mahachohan

① ② ③ ④ ⑤ ⑥ ⑦

Masters on the 7 rays

The Plan
The Masters know
the purpose

Higher mental

*Initiates and
world-servers*

The bodies of
the personality:

HUMANITY

Civilisations

- lower mental
- astral
- etheric-physical

The divine purpose
and plan are fulfil-
led and manifested
on Earth

Chart 2. The globe is a planatary system consisting of seven planes. Three big centres stimulate and create development on Earth: Shamballa, the Hierarchy and Humanity.

The Masters of the Hierarchy walked among men on Earth in the Atlantian days and these – to us humans – highly developed beings will come to Earth again to promote development.

The connection between the Hierarchy and Freemasonry

When it is stated that freemasonry was inspired from Sirius influence has come via the Hierarchy and the Masters and further to advanced human beings who have been able to grasp the ideas and who have been able to transform them into symbols and rituals to educate less developed humans.

The connection between the Hierarchy and freemasonry emerges from the following:

"I have made two affirmations during the past years anent the Hierarchy. One was that as a result of the cleansing of the Earth through the medium of the world war (1914-1945) and through the suffering to which humanity has been subjected (with a consequent purifying effect which will demonstrate later), it will be possible for the Hierarchy to externalise itself and function openly upon the physical plane. This will indicate a return to the situation which existed in Atlantean days when (using the Biblical symbolism) God Himself walked among men - divinity was present in physical form because the Members of the Hierarchy were guiding and directing the affairs of humanity as far as innate freewill permitted. On a higher turn of the spiral, this again will happen. The Masters will walk openly among men. Secondly, the Hierarchy will then restore the ancient Mysteries, the ancient landmarks so earnestly preserved by the Masonic tradition and which have been securely embalmed in the Masonic ritual, awaiting the day of resurrection.

These ancient Mysteries were originally given to humanity by the Hierarchy, and were - in their turn - received by the Hierarchy from the Great White Lodge on Sirius. They contain the clue to the evolutionary process, hidden in numbers and in words; they veil the secret of man's origin and destiny, picturing for him in rite and ritual the long, long path which he must tread. They provide also, when rightly interpreted and correctly presented, the teaching which humanity needs in order to progress from darkness to Light, from the unreal to the Real and from death to Immortality. Any true Mason who understands, even if only to a slight degree, the implications of that in which he participates will recognise this most ancient of Oriental prayers, giving the key to the three degrees of the Blue Lodge. I mention here the Masonic purpose because it is closely related to the restoration of the Mysteries and has held the clue - down the ages - to that long-awaited restoration, to the platform upon which the restored teaching can be based, and the structure which can express, in powerful ritual and in organised detailed rites, the history of man's moving forward upon the Path of Return.

The Mysteries will be restored in other ways also, for they contain much besides that which the Masonic rites can reveal or that religious rituals and ceremonies can disclose; they contain within their teaching and formulas the key to the science which will unlock the mystery of electricity - that mystery of which H.P.B. spoke; though much progress has already been made by science along this line, it is as yet only embryonic in nature, and only when the Hierarchy is present visibly on earth, and the Mysteries of which the Masters are the Custodians are given openly to man, will the true secret and nature of electrical phenomena be revealed.

The Mysteries are, in reality, the true source of revelation, and it can be only when the mind and the will-to-good are closely blended and conditioning human behaviour that the extent of the coming revelation will be grasped, for only then can humanity be trusted with these secrets. They concern those capacities which enable the Members of the Hierarchy to work consciously with the energies of the planet and of the solar system and to control forces within the planet; they will put the ordinary psychic powers (today so stupidly approached and so little understood) in their rightful place and guide man towards their helpful usage.

The Mysteries will restore colour and music as they essentially are to the world and do it in such a manner that the creative art of today will be to this new creative art what a child's building of wooden blocks is to a great cathedral such as Durham or Milan. The Mysteries, when restored, will make real - in a sense incomprehensible to you at present - the nature of religion, the purpose of science and the goal of education. These are not what you think today.

The ground is being prepared at this time for this great restoration. The Churches and Masonry are today before the judgment seat of humanity's critical mind and the word has gone forth from that mass mind that both of them failed in their divinely assigned tasks. It is realised everywhere that new life must be poured in and great changes wrought in the awareness and in the training of those who work through and in these two media of truth. Those changes have not yet been carried out, for it will take a new vision and a new approach to life experience, and this only the coming generation is capable of giving; they and they alone can bring about the needed alterations and the revitalisation, but it can and will be done:

"That which is a mystery shall no longer be so, and that which has been veiled will now be revealed: that which has been withdrawn will emerge into the light, and all men shall see and together they shall rejoice. That time will come when desolation has wrought its beneficent work, when all things have been destroyed, and men, through suffering, have sought to be impressed by that which they had discarded in vain pursuit of that which was near at hand and easy of attainment. Possessed, it proved to be an agency of death - yet men sought life, not death."

So runs *the Old Commentary* when referring to the present cycle through which mankind is passing." [5]

As it emerges there has been a connection between the Hierarchy and freemasons through time, and freemasons have via their rituals and symbols taught history of the evolution – in an esoteric sense, and they have preserved and passed on the facts about evolution, consciously or instinctively. As every freemason knows, evolution and creation are illustrated in every lodge. This is illustrated through symbols and rituals which are symbols or emblems of spiritual laws and truths. Everybody can learn to carry out the rituals in practice; the real work consists of *understanding the meaning and the significance* behind the symbols and rituals. Often the symbols can have distant and unfamiliar meanings. An example: Where do the two pillars come from and what do they mean? A distant and maybe unknown meaning is given as follows:

"I earlier gave a hint upon which definite astrological computation could be based when I gave the time of the "Great Approach" of the Hierarchy to our planetary manifestation when individualisation took place and the fourth kingdom in nature appeared. I placed that stupendous event as happening 21,688,345 years ago. At that time the Sun was in Leo.

The process then initiated upon the physical plane and producing outer physical events took approximately 5,000 years to mature and the Sun was in

Gemini when the final crisis of individualisation took place and the door was then closed upon the animal kingdom.

It has been stated that Sagittarius governs human evolution, as the Sun was in that sign when the Hierarchy began its Approach in order to stimulate the forms of life upon our planet. *Sagittarius, however, governed the period of the subjective approach.*

The Sun was in *Leo* when physical plane individualisation took place as a result of the applied stimulation.

The Sun was in *Gemini* when this Approach was consummated by the founding of the Hierarchy upon the Earth. This is one of the great secrets which the Masonic Rituals typify, for the symbol of the sign, Gemini, is the source of the concept of the two pillars, so familiar to Masons. It might therefore be stated that, symbolically speaking,

1. Leo governs the E.A. degree.
2. Gemini governs the F.C. degree.
3. Sagittarius governs the degree of M. M. up to the episode of the raising of the Master, and that Capricorn governs the final part of the ceremony and the H. R. A."[6]

Collaboration between Freemasonry and the Hierarchy in present time

You might easily presume that freemasonry and collaboration with the Hierarchy is something that belongs to the past. It took place in the past, it takes place in the present, and it will take place in the future. The Hierarchy works incessantly to stimulate and create the kingdom of God on Earth, and their collaboration-partners here on Earth are men of good will, worldservers and initiates. That is why it is crucial that there are men who dedicate themselves to this work in the present and in future.

Collaboration takes place every day – are we conscious or not, but the more consciousness we have in this work and the more actively we are able to collaborate, the more beneficial it will be and the more effectively we are able to contribute.

In the Aquarian age influences that will be flooding into us will help us to surrender to collaborate with the inner worlds, the Hierarchy and Shamballa. We will have the possibility of restoring the ancient mysteries, and we will get all the help and support that we wish from within.

"It is interesting to note that the seventh Ray of Ceremonial Law and Order works through Uranus which is today the transmitter of Sirian force via Pisces to the Hierarchy. From that "middle centre" it passes to that sensitive band of disciples, aspirants and workers to whose hearts and hands is committed the heavy task, incident to the re-organisation and the rebuilding of the shattered world structure. The seventh ray has sometimes been called a peculiar name by Knowers. It is regarded as the "Ray of Ritualistic Decency." It aids and inaugurates the appearing of a new world order, based on a spiritual drive and on aspiration, mental freedom, loving understanding and a physical plane rhythm which provides opportunity for full creative expression. To bring this about, energy from Shamballa (embodying the will-to-good) is fused and blended with the organising energy of the seventh ray and then carried to humanity along the stream of love which emanates from the Hierarchy itself. Pisces governs this effort of the Hierarchy because the highest aspect of Pisces which humanity can at this time in any way comprehend is that of Mediatorship. This is the energy of mediation, of right relationship. Today as never before the Hierarchy stands as a "mediating transmitter" between:

1. Humanity and the will of God. The revelation of the true significance and purpose of that will as it stands behind all world events is needed now as never before. This can come through a closer relation between the Hierarchy and Humanity.

2. Humanity and its karma, for it is equally essential that the laws for the transmutation of karma into active present good are clearly grasped.

3. Humanity and cosmic evil, focussed for many millenia of years in what has been called the Black Lodge. Speculation anent this Lodge and its activities is both fruitless and dangerous.

The latter fact is responsible for the widespread attack made upon Masonry during this century. Masonry - inadequate and corrupt as it has been and guilty of over-emphasising certain forms of symbols - is nevertheless a germ or seed of future hierarchical effort when that effort is - at some later date - externalised on Earth. Masonry is governed by the seventh ray, and when certain important changes have been made and the spirit of Masonry is grasped instead of the letter, then we shall see a new form of hierarchical endeavour appear to aid in the restoration of the ancient and sacred Mysteries among men."[7]

"As above so below"

"We are told that seven great rays exist in the cosmos. In our solar system only one of these seven great rays is in operation. The seven sub-divisions constitute the "seven rays" which, wielded by our solar Logos, form the basis of endless variations in His system of worlds. These seven rays may be described as the seven channels through which all being in His solar system flows, the seven predominant characteristics or modifications of life, for it is not to humanity only that these rays apply, but to the seven kingdoms as well. In fact there is nothing in the whole solar system, at whatever stage of evolution it may stand, which does not belong and has not always belonged to one or other of the seven rays."[8]

"The seven rays are the sum total of the divine Consciousness, of the universal Mind; They might be regarded as seven intelligent entities through Whom the plan is working out. They embody divine purpose, express the qualities required for the materialising of that purpose, and They create the forms and are the forms through which the divine idea can be carried forward to completion. Symbolically, They may be regarded as constituting the brain of the divine Heavenly Man. They correspond to the ventricles of the brain, to the seven centres within the brain, to the seven centres of force, and to the seven major glands which determine the quality of the physical body. They are the conscious executors of divine purpose; They are the seven Breaths, animating all forms which have been created by Them to carry out the plan.

It may perhaps be easier to understand the relation of the seven rays to Deity if we remember that man himself (being made in the image of God) is a seven-fold being, capable of seven states of consciousness, expressive of the seven principles or basic qualities which enable him to be aware of the seven planes upon which he is, consciously or unconsciously, functioning. He is a septenate at all times, but his objective is to be consciously aware of all the states of being, to express consciously all the qualities, and to function freely on all the planes.

The seven ray Beings, unlike man, are fully conscious and entirely aware of the purpose and the Plan. They are "ever in deep meditation," and have reached the point where, through Their advanced stage of development, They are "impelled toward fulfillment." They are fully self-conscious and group-conscious; They are the sum total of the universal mind; They are "awake and active." Their goal and Their purpose is such that it is idle for us to speculate about it, for the highest point of achievement for man is the lowest point for Them. These seven Rays, Breaths and Heavenly Men have the task of wrestling with matter in order to subjugate it to divine purpose, and the goal - as far as one can sense it - is to subject the material forms to the play of the life aspect, thus producing those qualities which will carry the will of God to completion. They are therefore the sum total of all the souls within the solar system, and Their activity produces all forms; according to the nature of the form so will be the grade of consciousness. Through the seven rays, the life or spirit aspect flows, cycling through every kingdom in nature and producing thus all states of consciousness in all fields of awareness."[9]

"As above ...." i.e. the Universe

The sun is part of a system on its own level, and at the same time the sun has its own system which we know as our solar system.

Chart 3 shows the Solar Logos in our system; Solar Logos is at the same time One and Three. The trinity of Solar Logos is referred to as the three aspects of the Deity, with the Christian terms as Father, Son and Holy Spirit. These three aspects influence the development on the planet through the first ray which transmits will-power, through the second ray which transmits love-wisdom and through the third ray which transmits active intelligence.

The aspect of the Holy Spirit or the third aspect unfolds through the four attribute rays, the fourth, the fifth, the sixth and the seventh ray. These rays unfold through harmony and beauty, concrete knowledge, devotion and idealism and the seventh through ceremony and organization.

Solar and Planetary Hierarchies

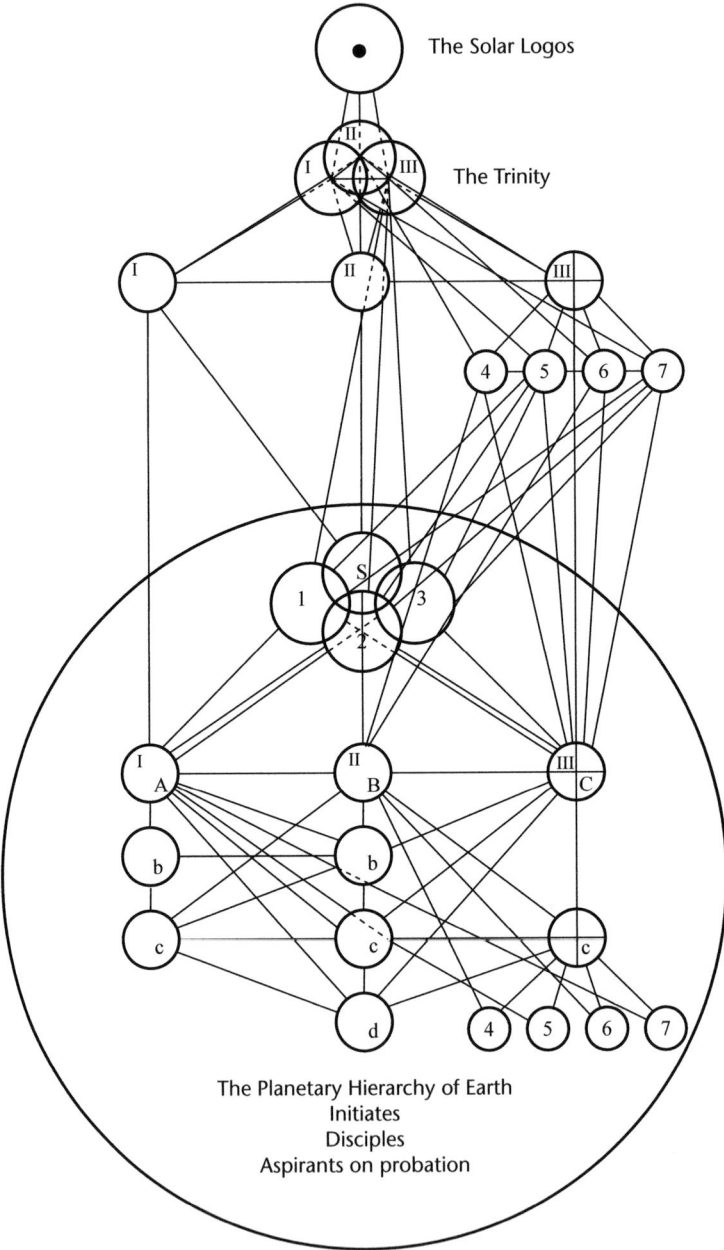

Chart 3. The survey shows how the Solar Hierarchy is connected to the Planetary Hierarchy.
The figures mentioned were the most prominent in the first half of the 20th century.

Key to diagram of Solar and Planetary Hierarchies

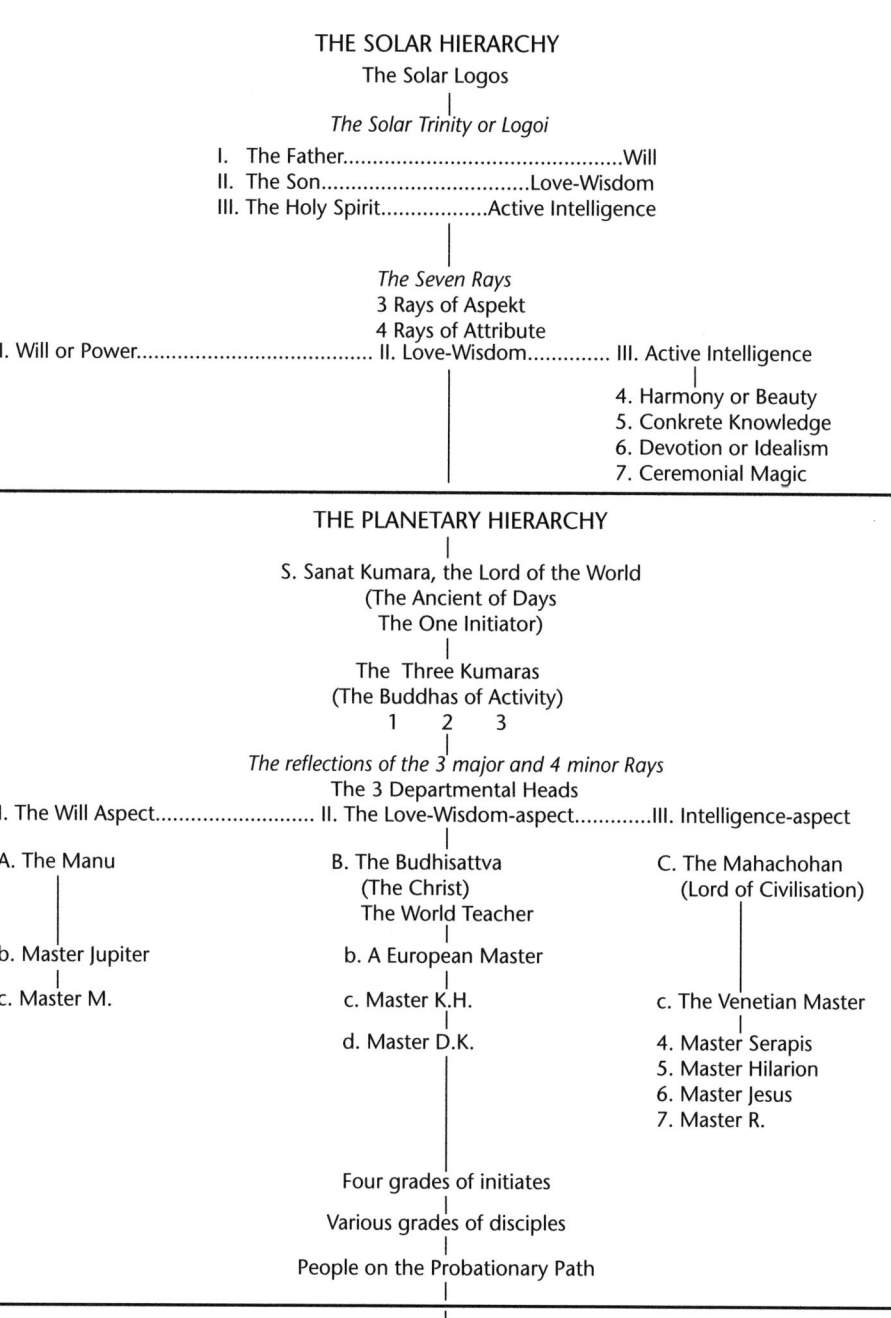

THE SOLAR HIERARCHY

The Solar Logos

The Solar Trinity or Logoi

I. The Father...Will
II. The Son..................................Love-Wisdom
III. The Holy Spirit.................Active Intelligence

The Seven Rays
3 Rays of Aspekt
4 Rays of Attribute

I. Will or Power.. II. Love-Wisdom.............. III. Active Intelligence

4. Harmony or Beauty
5. Konkrete Knowledge
6. Devotion or Idealism
7. Ceremonial Magic

THE PLANETARY HIERARCHY

S. Sanat Kumara, the Lord of the World
(The Ancient of Days
The One Initiator)

The Three Kumaras
(The Buddhas of Activity)
1   2   3

The reflections of the 3 major and 4 minor Rays
The 3 Departmental Heads

I. The Will Aspect.......................... II. The Love-Wisdom-aspect.............III. Intelligence-aspect

A. The Manu

B. The Budhisattva
(The Christ)
The World Teacher

C. The Mahachohan
(Lord of Civilisation)

b. Master Jupiter

b. A European Master

c. Master M.

c. Master K.H.

c. The Venetian Master

d. Master D.K.

4. Master Serapis
5. Master Hilarion
6. Master Jesus
7. Master R.

Four grades of initiates

Various grades of disciples

People on the Probationary Path

Average humanity of all degrees

Thus each ray has its specific name which refers to the energy of the ray which again develops special qualities in the various kingdoms.

The energy of the rays is transmitted through Solar Logos, and from the Solar Hierarchy the energies flow further into the hierarcal system of Earth. The system of the planet has a structure that corresponds to that of the Solar.

Highest in the hierarchy of Earth is the Lord of the World, Sanat Kumara - also called the Ancient of Days or the One Initiator. He works together with and through the three kumaras.

Sanat Kumara works through three planetary centres:
- the Manu governs the centre called Shamballa, the place where the will of God is known. The Manu has Masters to take care of the work.
- The World Teacher, the Bodhisattwa, governs the other centre that transmits love and wisdom. The World Teacher is Christ in present time. He also has a number of Masters to help with the work.
- The third centre is governed by the Mahachohan, also called the Lord of Civilization. This centre transmits the aspect of intelligence; it is from this point that the light from the mind of God streams into the mind of mankind so that humanity can illuminate Earth and fulfill Gods Plan on Earth. This centre is at present governed by the Master Rakoczy. In his department Masters are partly on the third ray and partly on the four attribute rays. Through his work life unfolds in the lower worlds.

A Treatise on Cosmic Fire mentioned a Venetian Master also referred to Mahachohan. Later informations that are given by the disciple Lucille Cedercrans say that Master Rakoczy has taken over this office.

On all rays there are several Masters each with specific tasks on their rays. Together they form the Hierarchy. These Masters all have special qualities which they have developed through evolution, and they are – like man – heading for higher phases of development.

".... so below" i.e. Man

The constitution of man is shown in chart 4 page 26-27. At the buttom of the chart is the personality of man consisting of three bodies: the physical-etheric body, the astral or emotional body and the lower mental body. The average man lives and is conscious on these three planes.

On the higher mental plane is seen the the soul of man, which the personality can contact through meditation.

The Higher Self is a triad consisting of spiritual mind, spiritual love-wisdom and spiritual will.

Through meditation man can build the antahkarana, a bridge from the lower mental unit to the higher mental permanent atom, and so he can become able to contact the Higher Self, the spiritual triad.

The Masters of Wisdom function in their spiritual triad.

On the monadic plane is the spirit of man which man will not be able to contact until an advanced stage on the path of evolution has been reached.

When man starts on his Path of Return to the Divine Source, he starts seeking inwards and upwards. He seeks away from the personal and material life and strives to raise his consciousness higher and higher inwards to get into contact with his own soul and with his own spirit.

There are three thing the seeker must do: cleanse himself from attachment to the tendencies and desires of the personality, meditate to create contact inwardly, and finally man must use his knowledge and his capacity to be of benefit and joy to humanity and kingdoms of Earth.

To get inspiration from the Hierarchy man must be able to raise his consciousness to the higher mental plane and further to the buddhic plane. That is where the Masters can be reached. The Masters work continuously and try incessantly to influence man, but only individuals who through meditation have built a channel from the personality inwards to the soul and to the Higher Self are able to grasp these signals from the Masters. And only individuals who have purified their emotional body and their lower mental body from selfish attachments will be able to grasp signals without too many veils so that in actual fact they are able to transform the signals into action according to the Plan.

The constitution of Man

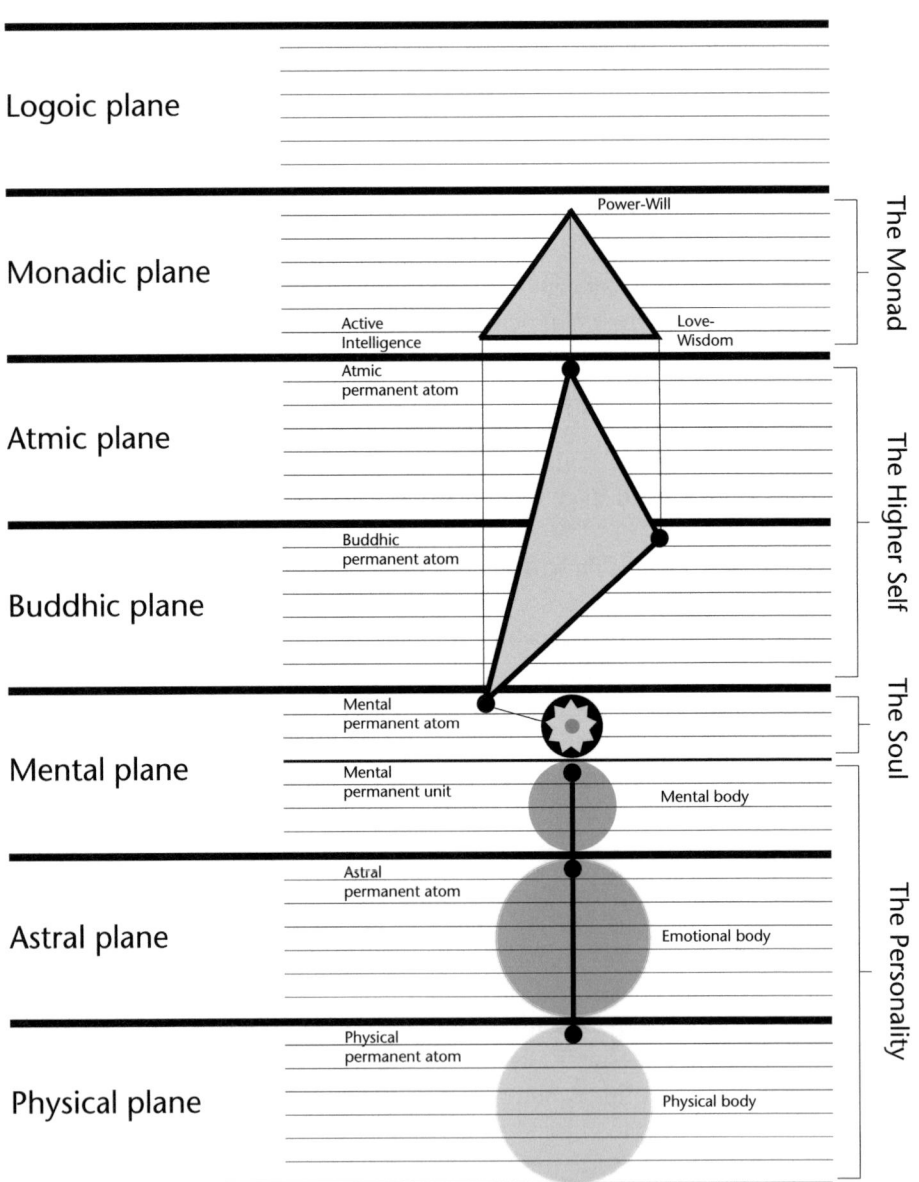

The constitution of Man.

The tripartition of Man

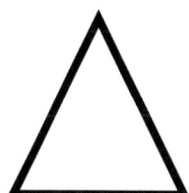

The Monad
Logoic germ
Biblical: Spirit

1. Divine Will

2. Divine Love-Wisdom

3. Divine Intelligence

The Monad reflects itself in the Higher Self
which is its instrument through the whole evolution

The Higher Self
The Higher Triad
Biblical: Soul

1. Atma - Spiritual Will

2. Buddhic- Spiritual Love-Wisdom

3. Manas - Spiritual Intelligence

The Higher Self manifests itself in the Soul or the Egoic Lotus,
which is its instrument through the whole realm of man.
The Soul reflects itself in the Personality,
which is its instrument through a whole incarnation.

The Personality
The Lower Triad
Biblical: Body

1. Lower mental body

2. Astral body

3. Physical-etheric body

From Piscean Age to Aquarian Age

Ages

The rays influence Earth and humanity in cycles. They manifest periodically and influence the evolution according to the Plan. The rays work via zodiac signs in cycles of 2000-2500 years which also mark one age.

In approximately 2000 years we have been influenced by the zodiac sign Pisces and the sixth ray. The sixth ray has reduced its power since 15-1600 A.D. and will be totally without influence circa 2500 A.D.

At the beginning of the 1600th century the seventh ray has been entering with the Aquarian age.

Around 2000 A.D. the influence from Aquarius will become stronger than that from Pisces, and thereafter the seventh ray will become more and more powerful and will influence humanity and evolution more and more.

To illustrate the connection between the immediate past to the immediate future following survey shows the influences of the sixth ray on the evolution and the influences that are to be expected under the seventh ray.

The 6th ray	The 7th ray
- The sixth ray influenced the astral body.	- The seventh ray will influence the physical body.
- The sixth ray fostered the vision.	- The seventh ray will materialize that which was visioned.

The 6th ray

- The sixth ray produced the mystic as its culminating type of aspirant.

- The sixth ray, as part of the evolutionary plan, led to separations, to nationalism, and to sectarianism, due to the selective nature of the mind and its tendency to divide and separate.

- The sixth ray activity led to the formation of bands of disciples, working in groups but not in close relation, and subject to internal dissension, based on personality reactions.

- The sixth ray brought the sense of duality to a humanity which regarded itself as a physical unity. Of this attitude the academic materialistic psychologists are the exponents.

The 7th ray

- The seventh ray will develop the magician who works in the field of white magic.

- The seventh ray will lead to fusion and synthesis, for its energy is of the type which blends spirit and matter.

- The seventh ray will train and send forth groups of initiates, working in close unison with the Plan and with each other.

- The seventh ray will inaugurate the sense of a higher unity; first, that of the integrated personality for the masses, and secondly, that of the fusion of soul and body for the world aspirants.

The 6th ray

- The sixth ray differentiates that aspect of the universal electrical energy which we know as modern electricity, produced to serve man's material needs.

- The sixth ray influence produced the emergence in men's minds of the following knowledges:
1. Knowledge of physical plane light and electricity.
2. Among the esotericists and spiritualists of the world, knowledge of the existence of the astral light.
3. An interest in illumination, both physical and mental.
4. Astro-physics and the newer astronomical discoveries.

The 7th ray

- The seventh ray period will familiarize man with that type of electrical phenomena which produce the coordination of all forms.

- The seventh ray will change the theories of the advanced thinkers of the race into the facts of the future educational systems. Education and the growth of the understanding of illumination in all fields will eventually be regarded as synonymous ideals.

The 6ᵗʰ ray

- The sixth ray taught the meaning of sacrifice, and of this teaching the crucifixion was the outstanding emblem, to the initiates. Philanthropy was the expression of the same teaching, to advanced humanity. The nebulous ideal of simply "being kind" is the same motivation, applied to the unthinking masses.

- The sixth ray promoted the growth of the spirit of individualism. Groups exist, but they are groups of individuals gathered around an individual.

- The sixth ray influence conveyed to men the ability to recognise the historical Christ, and to evolve the structure of the Christian faith, coloured by a vision of a great Son of Love, but qualified by an excessive militancy and separativeness, based on a narrow idealism.

The 7ᵗʰ ray

- The seventh ray will bring to the consciousness of the coming initiates the concept of group service and sacrifice. This will inaugurate the age of the "divine service". The vision of the giving of the individual in sacrifice and service, within the group and to the group ideal, will be the goal of the masses of advanced thinkers in the New Age, whilst for the rest of humanity, brotherhood will be the keynote of their endeavour. These words have a wider connotation and significance than the thinkers of today can know and understand.

- The seventh ray will foster the group spirit, and the rhythm of the group, the objectives of the group, and the ritual-working of the group will be the basic phenomena.

- The seventh ray will convey to man the power to recognise the cosmic Christ, and to produce that future scientific religion of Light which will enable man to fulfill the command of the historical Christ to permit his light to shine forth.

The 6th ray	The 7th ray

- The sixth ray produced the great idealistic religions with their vision and their necessary narrowness,—a narrowness that is needed to safeguard infant souls.

- The seventh ray will release the developed souls from the nursery stage and inaugurate that scientific understanding of the divine purpose which will foster the coming religious synthesis.

- The effect of the sixth ray influence has been to foster the separative instincts, - dogmatic religion, scientific factual accuracy, schools of thought with their doctrinal barriers and exclusiveness, and the cult of patriotism.

- The seventh ray will prepare the way for the recognition of the wider issues which will materialise as the new world religion which will emphasis unity but bar out uniformity; it will prepare for that scientific technique which will demonstrate the universal light that every form veils and hides, and for that internationalism which will express itself as practical brotherhood and as peace and goodwill between the peoples.
12

Freemasonry in the Aquarian Age

In the Aquarian age the seventh ray will influence the work of freemasonry deeply, because it will help in that:

A. *Many men will reach to the first initiation.*

"The seventh ray is, par excellence, the medium of relationship. It brings together the two fundamental aspects of spirit and matter. It relates soul and form and, where humanity is concerned, it relates soul and personality. In the first initiation, it makes the initiate aware of that relation; it enables him to take advantage of this "approaching duality" and - by the perfecting of the contact - to produce upon the physical plane the emergence into manifestation of the "new man." At the first initiation, through the stimulation brought about by seventh ray energy, the personality of the initiate and the hovering overshadowing soul are consciously brought together; the initiate then knows that he is - for the first time - a soul-infused personality. His task is now to grow into the likeness of what he essentially is. This development is demonstrated at the third initiation, that of the Transfiguration."[13]

B. *Man can function as an integrated personality.*

"*The integrationtechnique of the seventh ray*. However, the integration with which we shall primarily deal as we study the seven Techniques of Integration is that of the personality as it integrates into the whole of which it is a part, through service to the race and to the Plan. Bear in mind that *these ray techniques are imposed by the soul upon the personality after it has been somewhat integrated into a functioning entity* and is, therefore, becoming slightly responsive to the soul, the directing Intelligence."[14]

C. *Man can recognize himself as creator*

" It was the realisation of the present world need for illumined thinkers and subjective workers which prompted Those Who guide so to direct the incoming spiritual energies that the formation of the esoteric groups everywhere came about; it led also to the publication of the mass of mystical and Oriental literature on meditation and allied topics which has flooded the world today. Hence also the effort that I, a worker on the inner side of life, am making to teach the newer psychology in this treatise, and so show to man what is his equipment and how well suited he is to the work for which he has been created, and which he has as yet failed to comprehend. The force and the effect of the seventh ray influence will, however, reveal to him the magical work, and the next twenty five hundred years will bring about so much change and make possible the working of so many so-called "miracles" that even the outer appearance of the world will be profoundly altered; the vegetation and the animal life will be modified and developed, and much that is latent in the forms of both kingdoms will be brought into expression through the freer flow and the more intelligent manipulation of the energies which create and constitute all forms. The world has been changed beyond belief during the past five hundred years, and during the next two hundred years the changes will be still more rapid and deep-seated, for the growth of the intellectual powers of man is gathering momentum, and Man, the Creator, is coming into possession of His powers."[15]

D. *Humanity will become a channel for distributing of spiritual energy*

"One of the inevitable effects of seventh ray energy will be to relate and weld into a closer synthesis the four kingdoms in nature. This must be done as preparatory to the long fore-ordained work of humanity which is to be the distributing agency for spiritual energy to the three subhuman kingdoms. This is the major task of service which the fourth kingdom, through its incarnating souls, has undertaken. The radiation from the fourth kingdom will some day be so potent and far-reaching that its effects will permeate down into the very depths of the created phenomenal world, even into the mineral kingdom. Then we shall see the results to which the great initiate, Paul, refers when he speaks of the whole creation waiting for the manifestation of the Sons of God. That manifestation is that of radiating glory and power and love."[16]

E. *Man will recognize himself as part of a group*

"…. that one of the new things which the coming era of spiritual expansion will see is the inauguration of something entirely new: *Group Initiation*.

…. It must be remembered also that as humanity develops and more and more people begin to function as souls, the nature of the soul (which is relationship) begins to have an effect; men become larger in their outlook and their vision. The outlook of the separated self vanishes, and group relationship and group interest supersede that intense personal and interior relationship and interest which have made evolving man what he is: first of all an integrated personality, and then a disciple - a candidate for initiation. As more and more disciples come into group realisation it will become increasingly possible for the Hierarchy to admit such disciples in group formation. That is one reason necessitating the re-establishing of the Ancient Mysteries on Earth. That group relation has to be demonstrated in the three worlds and expressed by disciples in their group life upon the physical plane."[17]

"To sum up what I have said:

1. The energy of the seventh ray is the potent agent of initiation when taken on the physical plane, that is, during the process of the first initiation.

2. Its effect upon humanity will be:
   a. To bring about *the birth of the Christ-consciousness* among the masses of intelligently aspiring human beings.
   b. To set in motion certain relatively *new evolutionary processes* which will *transform humanity from 'world disciple' into humanity as 'world initiate'*.
   c. To establish in a new and intelligible manner the ever-existent sense of relationship and *thus bring about upon the physical plane right human relations.* The agent of this is goodwill, a reflection of the will-to-good of the first divine aspect. Of this first Ray of Will or Purpose, goodwill is the reflection.

d. *To readjust negative and positive relationships,* and - today - this will be carried forward primarily in connection with the sex relation and marriage.

e. *To intensify human creativity* and thus bring in the new art as a basis for the new culture and as a conditioning factor in the new civilisation.

f. *To reorganise world affairs and so initiate the new world order.* This is definitely in the realm of ceremonial magic.

3. The stimulation of this seventh ray will, in relation to the individual initiate,

a. *Bring into being upon the mental plane a widespread and recognized relation between the soul and the mind.*

b. *Produce a measure of order in the emotional processes of the initiate,* thus aiding the preparatory work of the second initiation.

c. Enable the initiate - upon the physical plane - *to establish certain service relationships, to learn the practice of elementary white magic, and to demonstrate the first stage of a truly creative life.*[18]

Revelation of the Mysteries

The energy that is overflowing Earth and humanity in the coming age will highly influence humanity in general and freemasonry in particular. Freemasonry works on the seventh ray which will unfold the divine life on the physical plane, and thus freemasonry might be of big use to evolution.

"Much that is here written and which is conveyed in these pages is in reality concerned with the appearance of the Kingdom of God - an appearance which can now take place because of three factors:

1. The growth of that Kingdom on Earth, and the thousands of people who recognise its laws and endeavour to live in accordance with its rules and spirit.
2. The fact that the signs of the time and the wide-spread need of humanity have evoked the Christ, and that He has decided to reappear.
3. The invocative cry of humanity is ascending hourly to "the secret place of the Most High" and the Hierarchy plans to emerge when Christ appears and restores the rule of the Spirit on Earth. The hour for the restoration of the ancient Mysteries has arrived.

These facts have been widely given out, during the past two years, as the result of the cleansing of the Earth through the medium of the world war (1914-1945) and through the suffering to which humanity has been subjected (with an equally potent purifying effect, which will demonstrate later). It will then be possible for the Hierarchy, the Church of Christ hitherto invisible, to externalise itself and to function openly upon the physical plane. This will indicate a return to the situation which existed in Atlantean days when (to use Biblical symbology, *Genesis* Chaps. 2 and 3) God Himself walked among men; He talked with them and there was no barrier between the Kingdom of men and the Kingdom of God. Divinity was then present in physical form and the Members of the spiritual Hierarchy were openly guiding and directing the affairs of humanity as far as man's innate freedom permitted. Now, in the immediate future, and on a higher turn of the spiral of life, this will again happen. The Masters will walk openly among men; the Christ will reappear in physical Presence. Another thing that will happen will be that the ancient Mysteries will be restored, the ancient landmarks will again be recognized - those landmarks which Masonry has so earnestly preserved and which have been hitherto securely embalmed in the Masonic rituals, waiting the day of restoration and of resurrection.

These ancient Mysteries were originally given to humanity by the Hierarchy and contain the entire clue to the evolutionary process, hidden in numbers, in ritual, in words and in symbology; these veil the secret of man's origin and destiny, picturing to him, in rite and ritual, the long, long path which he must tread, back into the light. They provide also (when rightly interpreted and correctly represented) the teaching which humanity needs in order to pass from darkness to Light, from the unreal to the Real and from death to Immortality. Any true Mason who understands, even if only to a slight degree, the significance of the three degrees of the Blue Lodge, and the implications of that in which he participates, will recognize the above three phrases for what they are, and will recognize the significance of the three degrees. I mention it here with Masonic purpose because it is closely related to the restoration of the Mysteries and has held the clue (down the ages) to that long awaited restoration, to the platform upon which the required teaching can be based and the structure which can express (when freed of its Jewish names and nomenclature, which are long out of date, though right three thousand years ago) the history of man's moving forward upon the Path of Return.

It is these Mysteries which Christ will restore upon His reappearance, thus reviving the churches in a new form, and restoring the hidden Mystery which they long have lost through their materialism. Masonry has also lost the true livingness it once possessed but, in its forms and rituals, the truth is preserved and can be recovered. This Christ will do. He will also revive these Mysteries in other ways; not all will seek the church or Masonry for the revitalising of their spiritual life. The true Mysteries will also reveal themselves through science and the incentive to search for them there will be given by the Christ. The Mysteries contain, within their formulas and teachings, the key to the science which will unlock the mystery of electricity - the greatest spiritual science and area of divine knowledge in the world, the fringes of which have only just been touched. Only when the Hierarchy is present visibly on Earth and the Mysteries of which the disciples of the Christ are the Custodians are given openly to the world, will the true secret and nature of electrical phenomena be revealed.

The Mysteries are, in the last analysis, the true source of revelation; it can only be when the mind and the will-to-good are closely fused and blended and are thus conditioning human behaviour that the extent of the coming revelation can be safely grasped. There are planetary energies and forces which men as yet cannot and do not control; they know nothing of them and yet upon them the life of the planet is dependent; they are also closely related to the despised psychic powers (today so stupidly approached and ignorantly used), yet these powers (when correctly assessed and used) will prove of enormous usefulness in the sciences which the Mysteries will reveal.

The Mystery of the Ages is, through the reappearance of the Christ, on the verge of revelation. Through the revelation of the soul that Mystery (which soul knowledge veils) will stand revealed. The Scriptures of the world have ever prophesied that, at the end of the age, we shall see the revelation of that which is secret and the emergence of that which has hitherto been concealed, into the light of day. As we know, our present cycle marks the end of the Piscean age; the next two hundred years will see the abolition of death or rather of our misconceptions as to death and the firm establishing of the fact of the soul's existence; the soul will then be known to be an entity and the motivating impulse and the spiritual force behind all manifested forms. The work of the Christ (two thousand years ago) was to proclaim certain great possibilities and the existence of great powers. His work when He reappears will be to prove the fact of these possibilities and to reveal the true nature and potency of man. The proclamation He made that we were all sons of God and own one universal Father will, in the near future, no longer be regarded as a beautiful, mystical and symbolic statement, but will be regarded as a proved scientific pronouncement. Our universal brotherhood and our essential immortality will be proven to be facts in nature.

The ground is being prepared at this time for the great restoration which the Christ will engineer. The world religions (including Christianity) and Masonry are today before the judgment seat of humanity's critical mind; the word has gone forth almost unanimously that both of them have failed in their divinely assigned tasks. It is realised everywhere that new life must be poured in, but this will take a new vision and a new approach to living conditions and this only the appearance of the Christ can teach and help us bring about. As an ancient Scripture says:

"That which has been a mystery shall no longer be so, and that which has been veiled will now be revealed; that which has been withdrawn will emerge into the light and will then enhance that light and all men will see and together will rejoice. The time will come when destruction will have wrought its beneficent work; then men, through suffering, will seek that which they have discarded. In vain pursuit, they sought that which was near at hand and easy of attainment. Possessed, they found that it proved an agency of death. Yet all the time, they sought for life, not death."

And the Christ will bring them life and life abundantly.

There is much talk these days concerning the mysteries of initiation. Every country is full of spurious teachers, teaching the so-called Mysteries, offering spurious initiations (usually at a cost and with a diploma) and misleading the people. Christ Himself taught that just before He came, this state of affairs would be found and that everywhere the false and the spurious would be proclaiming themselves. All this is, however, but indicative of His coming. The counterfeit ever guarantees the true. The talk, the discussions, the silly claim-making, the pseudo-occultism and the futile efforts to "take an initiation" (that undistinguished phrase which ignorant theosophical teachers have coined to express a deep spiritual experience) have been distinctive of the esoteric teaching ever since its modern inception in 1875. Then H.P. Blavatsky brought to the attention of the Western world the fact that great disciples and Masters of the Wisdom were present on the Earth, obedient to the guidance of the Christ. Later she deeply regretted doing this, as some of her papers, issued to her Esoteric Section, proclaimed. Yet what she did was all a part of the great plan and was no mistake. The interpretations and the excited reactions of the theosophists of her time were the mistake - a mistake which they have not yet acknowledged. This stupid reaction was aided and helped by the inquisitive nature of humanity itself, as well as by its aspiration which was undoubtedly aroused thereby. Men also, full of cupidity and commercial greed, exploited the theme and are still doing so.

The total effect of all these stupidities and errors of presentation has nevertheless been good. In all lands, men today are aware of the existence of the Masters and of the possibility offered and the opportunity presented to make *scientific* spiritual progress and thus become members of the Kingdom of God. This the churches had ignored and had - in the Victorian age particularly - looked upon science as an arch enemy.

All this flood of information about the mysteries of initiation - some of it indicative of a hidden truth, some of it the fabrications of an aspirational imagination and some commercially instigated - has definitely prepared humanity for the teaching it is believed Christ will give when again here with us in physical Presence.

Little as the orthodox Christian may care to admit it, the entire Gospel story in its four forms or presentations, contains little else except symbolic details about the Mysteries which are (as far as humanity is concerned) five in all. These Mysteries indicate, in reality, five important points in the spiritual history of an aspirant; they indicate also five important stages in the progress of human consciousness. This advance will become definite and clear in a manner not understood today, at some point during the Aquarian Age. Humanity, the world disciple (through its various groups all at various stages of unfoldment) will "enter into" new states of awareness and into new realms or spheres of mental and spiritual consciousness, during the next two thousand years.

Each age has left a reflection of a modern fivefold development upon it. Four ages have just passed away, astronomically speaking: Gemini, Taurus, Aries, and Pisces. Today Aquarius, the fifth age, is coming into power. In Gemini, its symbolical sign of the two pillars set its seal upon the Masonic Fraternity of the time and the two pillars of Jachin and Boaz - to give them their Jewish names which are, of course, not their real names - came into being approximately eight thousand years ago. Then came Taurus, the Bull, wherein Mithra came as the world Teacher and instituted the Mysteries of Mithras with an (apparent) worship of the Bull. Next followed Aries the Ram, which saw the start of the Jewish Dispensation which is of importance to the Jews and unfortunately of importance to the Christian religion, but of no importance to the untold millions in the other parts of the world; during this cycle came the Buddha, Shri Krishna and Sankaracharya; finally we have the age of Pisces the Fishes, which brought to us the Christ. The sequence of the Mysteries which each of the signs of the Zodiac embodies will be clarified for us by the Christ, because the public consciousness today demands something more definite and spiritually real than modern astrology, or all the pseudo-occultism so widely extant.

In the era which lies ahead, after the reappearance of the Christ, hundreds of thousands of men and women everywhere will pass through some one or other of the great expansions of consciousness, but the mass reflection will be that of the renunciation (though this does not mean that the masses will by any means take the fourth initiation); they will renounce the materialistic standards which today control in every layer of the human family. One of the lessons to be learnt by humanity at the present time (a time which is the ante-chamber to the new age) is how few material things are really necessary to life and happiness. The lesson is not yet learnt. It is, however, essentially one of the values to be extracted out of this period of appalling deprivations through which men are every day passing. The real tragedy is that the Western Hemisphere, particularly the United States, will not share in this definite spiritual and vitalising process; they are at present too selfish to permit it to happen.

You can see, therefore, that initiation is not a ceremonial procedure, or an accolade, conferred upon a successful aspirant; neither is it a penetration into the Mysteries - of which the mysteries of Masonry are, as yet, only the pictorial presentation - but is simply the result of experiencing "livingness" on all three levels of awareness (physical, emotional and mental) and - through that livingness - bringing into activity those registering and those recording cells within the brain substance which have hitherto not been susceptible to the higher impression. Through this expanding area of registration or, if you prefer it, through the development of a finer recording instrument or responsive apparatus, the mind is enabled to become the transmitter of higher values and of spiritual understanding. Thus the individual becomes aware of areas of divine existence and of states of consciousness which are always eternally present but which the individual man was constitutionally unable to contact or to register; neither the mind, nor its recording agent, the brain, were able to from the angle of their evolutionary development.

When the searchlight of the mind is penetrating slowly into hitherto unrecognised aspects of the divine mind, when the magnetic qualities of the heart are awakening and becoming sensitively responsive to both the other aspects, then the man becomes able to function in the new unfolding realms of light, love and service. He is initiate.

These are the mysteries with which the Christ will deal; His acknowledged Presence with us and the presence of His disciples will make possible a far more rapid development than would otherwise be the case. The stimulation of the objective Hierarchy will be increasingly potent and the Aquarian Age will see so many of the sons of men accepting the great Renunciation that world effort will be on the same scale as the mass education of mankind in the Piscean Age. *Materialism as a mass principle will be rejected* and the major spiritual values will assume greater control.

The culmination of a civilisation, with its special note, quality and gifts to posterity, is significant of the reflection of the spiritual intent, and (through its massed populations) of one of the initiations. History will some day be based and written upon the record of the initiatory growth of humanity; prior to that, we must have a history which is constructed around the development of humanity under the influences of great and fundamental ideas. That is the next historical presentation.

The production of the culture of any given period is simply the reflection of the creative ability and the precise consciousness of the initiates of the time - those who knew they were initiate and were also conscious of admittance into direct relation with the Hierarchy. At present, we use neither of these two words, civilisation and culture, in their rightful sense or with their true meaning. Civilisation is the reflection in the mass of men of some particular cyclic influence, leading to an initiation. Culture is esoterically related to those within any era of civilisation who specifically, precisely and in full waking consciousness, through self-initiated effort, penetrate into those inner realms of thought activity which we call the creative world. These are the realms which are responsible for the outer civilisation.

The reappearance of the Christ is indicative of a closer relation between the outer and the inner worlds of thought. The world of meaning and the world of experience will be obviously blended through the stimulation of the advent of the Hierarchy and of its Head, the Christ. A tremendous growth of understanding and of relationships will be the major result."[19]

Education in the New Age

It is pointed out things that prevent men from coming forth to initiation, and there are things that prevent men from being of any use to the Hierarchy.

One obstacle is that human beings are deficient in reaching the causal level and in acquiring the consciousnes of the causal level. Human beings are certainly about to understand the meaning of meditation, and teaching in concentration and mental development is taking place everywhere. In the future it might provide a basis of the work so that men can understand what real meditation is.

Another obstacle is the widespread resistance to accept training and scientific development of the bodies.

To make human beings qualified for functioning as the extension of the Hierarchy on Earth, and to get men getting the knowledge and the inner connection that is necessary, it again and again is pointed out the importance of training of each individual man. A training where the human being become acquainted with himself by acquiring knowledge of mans constitution and developing the bodies, learn meditation and develop contact to the soul. This should be done out of the motto: *Man, know youself!*

Contemporary with knowledge and inner education of man himself, he shall acquire knowledge of cosmos and understanding of coherence out of the motto: *That which is above is that which is below!*

Through this training man will arrive to his true ego, the inner godman can be realized, and mans true purpose on Earth can be experienced.

"Mental development when paralleled by emotional stability and a strong healthy body is the aim for all. But now you have mental development paralleled by an unstable astral and a weak, underfed, badly raised physical.

Hence disorder, lack of balance, the clouding of the vision and disproportionate discussion. Lower mind, instead of being a means to achieve a goal and a tool to use, is becoming a ruler and a tyrant preventing the intuition from playing freely. Likewise the abstract conscious mind is cut off.

Hence the Masters, if it can in any way be accomplished, propose a movement that has in view the harnessing of the lower mind through the instrumentality of the people themselves. With this object in view They plan to utilise the incoming Ray of Ceremonial Law or Organisation, and the period immediately co-incident or following the coming of the Great Lord, to start these schools (in a small inconspicuous way at first) and bring to the consciousness of men everywhere the following four fundamentals:

a. The evolutionary history of man from the *mental* side.
b. The septenary constitution of the macrocosm and the microcosm.
c. The laws governing man's being.
d. The method of occult development.

A beginning has already been made through the various schools at present extant.
..... All these are the beginnings of the plan. When they are firmly grounded, when they are working smoothly and with public recognition, and when the world of men is being somewhat coloured by them and their *subjective* emphasis, when they are producing scholars and workers, politicians and scientists and educational leaders who make their impress on their environment, then maybe will come the time for the founding in exoteric fashion of the true occult school. By that I mean that if the earlier schools and colleges do their work satisfactorily they will have demonstrated to the world of men that *the subjective is the true reality* and that the lower is but the stepping stone to the higher. This subjective reality being universally admitted will, therefore, permit of the founding of a chain of inner schools .... that will be publicly recognized. This will never at any time obviate the necessity for always having an esoteric and secret section, for always there will be certain truths and facts of dangerous import to the uninitiated; but what I seek to point out is that the mysteries will eventually be admitted as facts for universal recognition and for universal aim and goal. They will be prepared for and entered from schools that definitely undertake, under expert guidance, to train novitiates for the mysteries.
.....

H. P. B. laid the foundation stone of the first school in this particular lesser cycle (which is nevertheless a relatively important one, being an outgrowth of the fifth root-race, the efflorescence of the fifth principle). This is the keystone. The work proceeds in the founding, as aforesaid, of the various schools, and mental science also has its place. It will go forward as desired if each one who is now under occult training strains every nerve and bends every effort to the work in hand. If all that is possible is done, when the Great Lord comes with His Masters the work will receive a still further impetus, and will gradually expand and grow till it becomes a power in the world. Then will come the day of the occult schools that will definitely train men for initiation."[20]

It is mentioned that preparing schools will be established, also known as occult fundamental schools. They will be governed from Shamballa, and the Hierarchy will be at the head of the education, disciplining and training. Of course all work will be in accordance with the spiritual laws and rules.

"The one fundamental school may be recognized by certain outstanding characteristics:

1. By the basic character of the truths taught as embodied in the following postulates:

   a. The unity of all life.
   b. The graded steps of development as recognised in man, and by the graded steps of its curriculum, which lead a man from one expansion of consciousness to another until he has reached that which we call perfection.
   c. The relationship between the microcosm and the macrocosm and its sevenfold application.
   d. The method of this development and the place of the microcosm within the macrocosm as revealed through the study of the periodicity of all manifestation and the basic law of cause and effect.

2. By the emphasis laid on character building and spiritual development as a foundation for the development of all the faculties inherent in the mirocosm.

3. By the requirement, demanded of all affiliated pupils without exception, that the life of inner unfoldment and development should be paralleled by a life of exoteric service.

4. By the graded expansions of consciousness that are the result of the imparted training; these lead a man on from step to step till he contacts his higher self, his Master, his egoic group, the First Initiator, the One Paramount Initiator, until he has contacted the Lord of his Ray and has entered into the bosom of his "Father Which is in Heaven"."[21]

The occult fundamental schools appear various places in the world; one of the lines will have its headquarters in the west, and behind them the Master Rakoczy (the seventh ray) and one of the English Masters work together with the Master Hilarion (fifth ray).

To be qualified to these schools seekers are requested to study with greater aspiration and to work with stronger enthusiasm. The Aspirant is requested to:

- aspire to realize the divine in everybody. In that way true occult obdience will be promoted and developed because it is not based on the personality, but on an instinctive realization of the inner Master

- to aspire to think in groupterms and do it on your own without being addicted to the words from others, to get to clarity

- to aspire to cleanse and purify the bodies and make them reliebe servers

- to aspire to equip the mental body

- to practise stringent self-discipline

As mentioned before all education and teaching will be organized and carried out according to the cosmic lows.[22]

The student must deal with:

The Law of Economy, that primarily governs man's instinct nature,
The Law of Attraction, that governs the soul-aspect of man and of all
               lifeforms from atom to a solar-system
and *the Law of Synthesis* which will guide man when he has arrived to the
               Path of Initiation, but which still only means very
               little to him.

To give a glimpse of the extent of the studies the following is quoted:

"Besides these three there are seven other laws that we might consider secondary laws, and which bring forth the evolutionary development of man, the personality, and of man, the soul. They are the following:

1. The Law of Vibration, the atomic law of the solar system
2. The Law of Cohesion, an aspect of the Law of attraction
3. The Law of Disintegration,
4. The Law of Magnetic Control which hides the control of the personality by the Monad via the egoic body.
5. The Law of Fixation by which the mind controls and stabilises, and cohereney is the result.
6. The Law of Love which aims at the transmutation of the desire nature.
7. The Law of Sacrifice and Death."[23]

"These seven laws concern the form side of life. To these ten laws must be added the seven laws of the soul which we are here considering. These begin to play upon the man and produce his more rapid spiritual unfoldment after he has been subjected to the discipline of the Probationary Path, or the Path of Purification. He is then ready to tread the final stages of the Path.

These seven laws are the basis of all true psychological understanding and, when their influence is better grasped, man will arrive at real self knowledge. He will then be ready for the fourth initiation which releases him from all further need for rebirth. This is the truth which underlies the Masonic teaching, which is given under the symbolism of the first eighteen degrees. These can be divided into four groups of degrees: Entered Apprentice, Fellow Craft, (followed by the Mark degree) Master Mason (followed by the H.R.A.) and the grouped degrees, four to seventeen, in the Scottish Rite. These seventeen degrees prepare the man for the fourth or fundamental degree, taken by a man who is a Master Mason. It can only be taken when the Master is in possession of the true Lost Word. He has risen from the dead; he has been entered, passed, and raised, and now can be perfected. Herein lies a great mystery. These seventeen degrees, leading to the first great step, (taken by the risen Master) are subjectively related to the seventeen laws which we have been considering. There is a parallelism worth noting between:

1. The eighteen laws:
   a. The three major laws of the universe,
   b. The seven minor laws of the solar system,
   c. The seven basic laws of the soul, plus what we might call the great law of Deity Itself, the law of God's synthetic purpose.

2. The eighteen subplanes through which man makes his way:
   a. The seven physical subplanes.
   b. The seven astral or emotional-desire subplanes.
   c. The four lower mental subplanes.

3. The eighteen degrees in Masonry, from that of the Entered Apprentice to that of the perfected initiate of the Rose Croix Chapter.

4. The eighteen centres of force with which the spiritual man has to work:
   a. The seven centres in the etheric body.
   b. The seven centres in the astral body.
   c. The three rows of petals in the egoic lotus.
   d. The "Jewel in the Lotus", at the heart of the "flower of the soul", which makes the eighteenth centre.

An understanding of these symbolic relations will do much to clarify the way of the soul in a body, and will constitute the basis of all true esoteric psychological study."[24]

The occult fundamental schools will give focus on three things: *Meditation, studies and service.* The three things shall be worked on separately, and at the same time they shall be foundation for each other and reciprocally support and develop each other.

It has been pointed out that the three great sciences which in the New Age will lead humanity *from the unreal to the Real and from aspiration to Realization* are:

"1. The science of Meditation, the coming science of the mind.
2. The science of Antahkarana, or the science of the bridging which must take place between higher and lower mind.
3. The science of Service, which is a definite technique of at-one-ment."[25]

Teaching in the New Age

The development of human beings through evolution has moved *from instinct to intellect*, and the next ability to be developed is *intuition*.

During the age that we are now leaving education has emphasized development of intellect. This has resulted in humanity now being enabled to use its mental tool and has further resulted in an enormous development of our society.

In the coming age mental ability shall still be developed, and in addition humanity will be trained in developing skills of *intuition.*

Teaching through symbols

In freemasonry symbols and rituals are employed in the teaching.

A symbol is an outer and visible form of an inner and spiritual reality. A symbol reflects objects from higher planes. Symbols are a picture-alphabet which has been used by initiates to illustrate and pass on spiritual states.

Symbols exist in *the world of the personality*. They are reflections through which the student is able to learn and acquire knowledge of the spiritual world. Through this work the student will find the *meaning* behind the symbols. *The meaning is in the world of the soul.* Finally the student by entering still deeper behind the veils may discover the *significance*. *The significance is in the world of the spirit.*

Working with symbols consists of three stages:

1. Exoterical study of the symbol that involves analysis of its form, lines, colour etc. Then you try to grasp the quality of the symbol in the

emotional body from a sensitive respons of its qualitative nature's influence. Finally you consider the inherent idea, its educational purpose and the intelletual meaning. This study takes place *on the level of the personality* and with its bodies.

2.   An intuitive perception of the symbol. This stage aims at a synthetic understanding of the purpose of the symbol, of its position in an organized manifest plan and its entire intention. This is regarded into the divine manifestation. This study takes place *on the level of the soul* through meditation.

3.   At this stage you identify yourself with the quality and the intention of the symbol. The symbol "is to be held continuously in the light" when it is to be enlightened in the mind. Thus the purpose and the intention may be grasped. This leads to magnetization of the symbol with the necessary quality, so that the intuitively grasped and qualified idea may find an appropriate form on the physical level. From the level of the soul consciousness is raised to *the level of the spirit* where the intention and plan of the spirit may be grasped. These are then brought back to the brain-consciousness which can transform the intention in the physical world.

Working with *symbols on the level of the personality takes place through mental studies and observations via the five senses.*

The method to understand inherent meaning is meditation, and as the student through meditation develops contact with the soul, meaning will be revealed to him.

After this – when the student *has* achieved soul-contact and he *has* built the antahkarana – he will attain even deeper contact, and here a higher initiate will reveal *the world of significance, the world of reality and the world of essential truth.*

When the student *has* done his work and has achieved the last mentioned stage, the world of significance, there will be help from within:

SYMBOL	MEANING	SIGNIFICANCE
Personality	Soul	Spirit
The world of occurrences	The world of transmission	The world of purpose
Appearance	Quality	Life
Symbol: Crescent moon	Symbol: Light - light shining on the Pathway of man and illuminating occurrences and granting revelations	Symbol: The five-pointed star and the radiant heart of the sun

Chart 5

"I would point that it is not his task to reveal the world of symbols. The five senses and the mind principle are adequate to bring that about. It is not his task to reveal the world of meaning. That, the disciple arrives at and interprets as he develops soul consciousness. His is the task to reveal the world of significances, the world of reality and of essential truth. Because of the success of the evolutionary process, this latter task is growing, and more and more initiated revealers will be needed during the period immediately ahead. Forget not that the invocative appeal of the mass of men, and the intelligent voicing of demand by those prepared intelligently to move forward, will inevitably call forth the needed response and the needed revealers of reality."[27]

Knowledge, wisdom and understanding

Another way of illustrating education is by regarding the concepts: *Knowledge, wisdom and understanding.*

"It might be of benefit to us also if we studied first the difference or the connection between *Knowledge, Understanding, and Wisdom.* Though in ordinary parlance they are frequently interchanged, as used technically they are dissimilar.

Knowledge is the product of the Hall of Learning. It might be termed the sumtotal of human discovery and experience, that which can be recognised by the five senses, and be correlated, diagnosed, and defined by the use of the human intellect. It is that about which we feel mental certitude, or that which we can ascertain by the use of experiment. It is the compendium of the arts and sciences. It concerns all that deals with the building and developing of the form side of things. Therefore it concerns the material side of evolution, matter in the solar systems, in the planet, in the three worlds of human evolution, and in the bodies of men.

Wisdom is the product of the Hall of Wisdom. It has to do with the development of the life within the form, with the progress of the spirit through those ever-changing vehicles, and with the expansions of consciousness that succeed each other from life to life. It deals with the life side of evolution. Since it deals with the essence of things and not with the things themselves, it is the intuitive apprehension of truth apart from the reasoning faculty, and the innate perception that can distinguish between the false and the true, between the real and the unreal. It is more than that, for it is also the growing capacity of the Thinker to enter increasingly into the mind of the Logos, to realise the true inwardness of the great pageant of the universe, to vision the objective, and to harmonise more and more with the higher measure. For our present purpose (which is to study somewhat the Path of Holiness and its various stages) it may be described as the realisation of the "Kingdom of God within," and the apprehension of the "Kingdom of God without" in the solar system. Perhaps it might be expressed as the gradual blending of the paths of the mystic and the occultist, - the rearing of the temple of wisdom upon the foundation of knowledge.

KNOWLEDGE	UNDERSTANDING	WISDOM
In the Hall of Learning	⟷	In the Hall of Wisdom
Science of Matter		Science of the Spirit
Objective	The Relation between Knowledge and Wisdom	Subjective
Dividing		Creating synthesis
Separates and Differentiates	⟷	Unites and Blends
Relation to the not-self		Relation to the Self

Chart 6

Wisdom is the science of the spirit, just as knowledge is the science of matter. Knowledge is separative and objective, whilst wisdom is synthetic and subjective. Knowledge divides; wisdom unites. Knowledge differentiates whilst wisdom blends. What, then, is meant by the understanding?

The understanding may be defined as the faculty of the Thinker in Time to appropriate knowledge as the foundation for wisdom, that which enables him to adapt the things of form to the life of the spirit, and to take the flashes of inspiration that come to him from the Hall of Wisdom and link them to the facts of the Hall of Learning. Perhaps the whole idea might be expressed in this way:

Wisdom concerns the one Self, knowledge deals with the not-self, whilst the understanding is the point of view of the Ego, or Thinker, or his relation between them.

In the Hall of Ignorance the form controls, and the material side of things has the predominance. Man is there polarised in the personality or lower self. In the Hall of Learning the higher self, or Ego, strives to dominate that form until gradually a point of equilibrium is reached where the man is controlled entirely by neither. Later the Ego controls more and more, until in the Hall of Wisdom it dominates in the three lower worlds, and in increasing degree the inherent divinity assumes the mastery."[28]

If education is going to consider everybody, work must include *knowledge, wisdom and understanding.*

If education is going to support the development of the *entire* human being, it must consider the needs of knowledge of the aspirants or the disciples. This is done through traditional studies.

If the needs of the aspirants or the disciples of developing wisdom are to be considered, meditation must be taught and practised.

Finally education has to give options to experience the acquired knowledge in various ways so that the aspirant and disciple are enabled to develop their understanding further.

A true Master Builder

""Let the Temple of the Lord be built", the seventh great Angel cried. Then to their places in the north, the south, the west and east, seven great sons of God moved with measured pace and took their seats. The work of building thus began.

The doors were closed. The light shone dim. The temple walls could not be seen. The seven were silent and their forms were veiled. The time had not arrived for the breaking forth of light. The Word could not be uttered. Only between the seven Forms the work went on. A silent call went forth from each to each. Yet still the temple door stayed shut.

As time went on, the sounds of life were heard. The door was opened, and the door was shut. Each time it opened, the power within the temple grew; each time the light waxed stronger, for one by one the sons of men entered the temple, passed from north to south, from west to east and in the centre of the heart found light, found understanding and the power to work. They entered through the door; they passed before the Seven; they raised the temple's veil and entered into life.

The temple grew in beauty. Its lines, its walls, its decorations, and its height and depth and breadth slowly emerged and entered into light.

Out from the east, the Word went forth: Open the door to all the sons of men who come from all the darkened valleys of the land and seek the temple of the Lord. Give them the light. Unveil the inner shrine, and through the work of all the craftsmen of the Lord extend the temple's walls and thus irradiate the world. Sound forth the Word creative and raise the dead to life.

Thus shall the temple of the light be carried from heaven to earth. Thus shall its walls be reared upon the great plains of the world of men. Thus shall the light reveal and nurture all the dreams of men.

Then shall the Master in the east awaken those who are asleep. Then shall the warden in the west test and try all the true seekers after light. Then shall the warden in the south instruct and aid the blind. Then shall the gate into the north remain wide open, for there the unseen Master stands with welcoming hand and understanding heart, to lead the pilgrims to the east where the true light shines forth.

"Why this opening of the temple?" demand the greater Seven. Because the work is ready; the craftsmen are prepared. God has created in the light. His sons can now create. What can else be done?"

"Naught!" came the answer from the greater Seven. "Let the work proceed. Let the sons of God create."

These words will be noted by many as of deep significance and as indicating a wide intention (during the coming cycle) to open the door wide into the temple of the hidden mystery to man. One by one we shall undergo the esoteric and spiritual counterpart of the psychological factor which is called "a mental test." That test will demonstrate a man's usefulness in mental work and power, it will show his capacity to build thought-forms and to vitalise them. This I dealt with in *A Treatise on White Magic,* and the relation of that treatise to the magical work of the seventh ray and its cycle of activity will become increasingly apparent. *A Treatise on White Magic* is an attempt to lay down the rules for training and for work which will make it possible for the candidate to the mysteries to enter the temple and to take his place as a creative worker and thus aid in the magical work of the Lord of the Temple."[29]

The creative work is governed by the Lord of the Seventh Ray.
"This ray Lord has a peculiar power on earth and on the physical plane of divine manifestation. His usefulness to His six Brothers is therefore apparent. He makes Their work appear. He is the most active of all the rays in this world period, and is never out of manifestation for more than fifteen hundred years. It is almost as if He whirled in and out of active work under a very rapid cycle, and His closest relation, symbolically, is to His Brethren of the second and fifth

rays in this world period.

He builds (using second ray cooperation) through the power of thought (thus cooperating with the Lord of the fifth ray and on the physical plane, which is His own essential and peculiar sphere). In another world period His relation with the other ray Lords may undergo change, but at this time His work will be more easily understood when He is recognised as aiding the building Lord of the second ray and utilising the energies of the Lord of concrete thought."[30]

Each of the seven rays govern their own plane in cosmos so that the first ray governs the first plane, the second ray governs the second plane etc. and the seventh governs the seventh and the physical plane.

So when the Creator creates his universe, the impuls emanates from the highest plane and descends through the planes into our planetary system to Shamballa where the will of God is known, to the Hierarchy and further to humanity. Here developed souls grasp the idea and manifestate it in the physical. See chart 2 page 14

The seventh ray is the energy of Ceremonial Order. "It is an expression of the will which drives through into outer manifestation; it is that which embodies both the periphery and the point at the centre. It is the will to "ritualistic synthesis," if I might so word it. It is Necessity which is the prime conditioning factor of the divine nature - the necessity to express itself; the necessity to manifest in an orderly rhythmic manner; the necessity to embrace "that which is above and that which is below" and, through the medium of this activity, to produce beauty, order, perfect wholes and right relationships. It is the driving energy which Being emanates as It appears and takes form and lives. It is the Will towards Expression. Today, as regards humanity, its highest expression is organisation."[31]

When man is able to understand his own inner reality he will be in his own power and become a true creator in the world.
" It was the realisation of the present world need for illumined thinkers and subjective workers which prompted Those Who guide so to direct the incoming spiritual energies that the formation of the esoteric groups everywhere came about; it led also to the publication of the mass of mystical and Oriental literature on meditation and allied topics which has flooded the world today. Hence also the effort that I, a worker on the inner side of life, am making to teach the

newer psychology in this treatise, and so show to man what is his equipment and how well suited he is to the work for which he has been created, and which he has as yet failed to comprehend. The force and the effect of the seventh ray influence will, however, reveal to him the magical work, and the next twenty five hundred years will bring about so much change and make possible the working of so many so-called "miracles" that even the outer appearance of the world will be profoundly altered; the vegetation and the animal life will be modified and developed, and much that is latent in the forms of both kingdoms will be brought into expression through the freer flow and the more intelligent manipulation of the energies which create and constitute all forms. The world has been changed beyond belief during the past five hundred years, and during the next two hundred years the changes will be still more rapid and deep-seated, for the growth of the intellectual powers of man is gathering momentum, and Man, the Creator, is coming into possession of His powers."[32]

"When the light of the seven Rays is blended with the seventh Ray, then Light Supernal can be known." [33]

The stages of the buildingproces

In order to become a true master builder the six stages of the building-proces must be mastered.

The six stages of the building-proces are:

1. Intention
2. Visualization
3. Projections
4. Invocation and evocation
5. Stabilization
6. Resurrection

"The three preceding stages mark, in reality, the three stages of personality work. The remaining three are expressions of response from higher levels of the spiritual life; beyond briefly indicating them, there is very little that I can put into words. The task of Invocation, based on Intention, Visualisation and

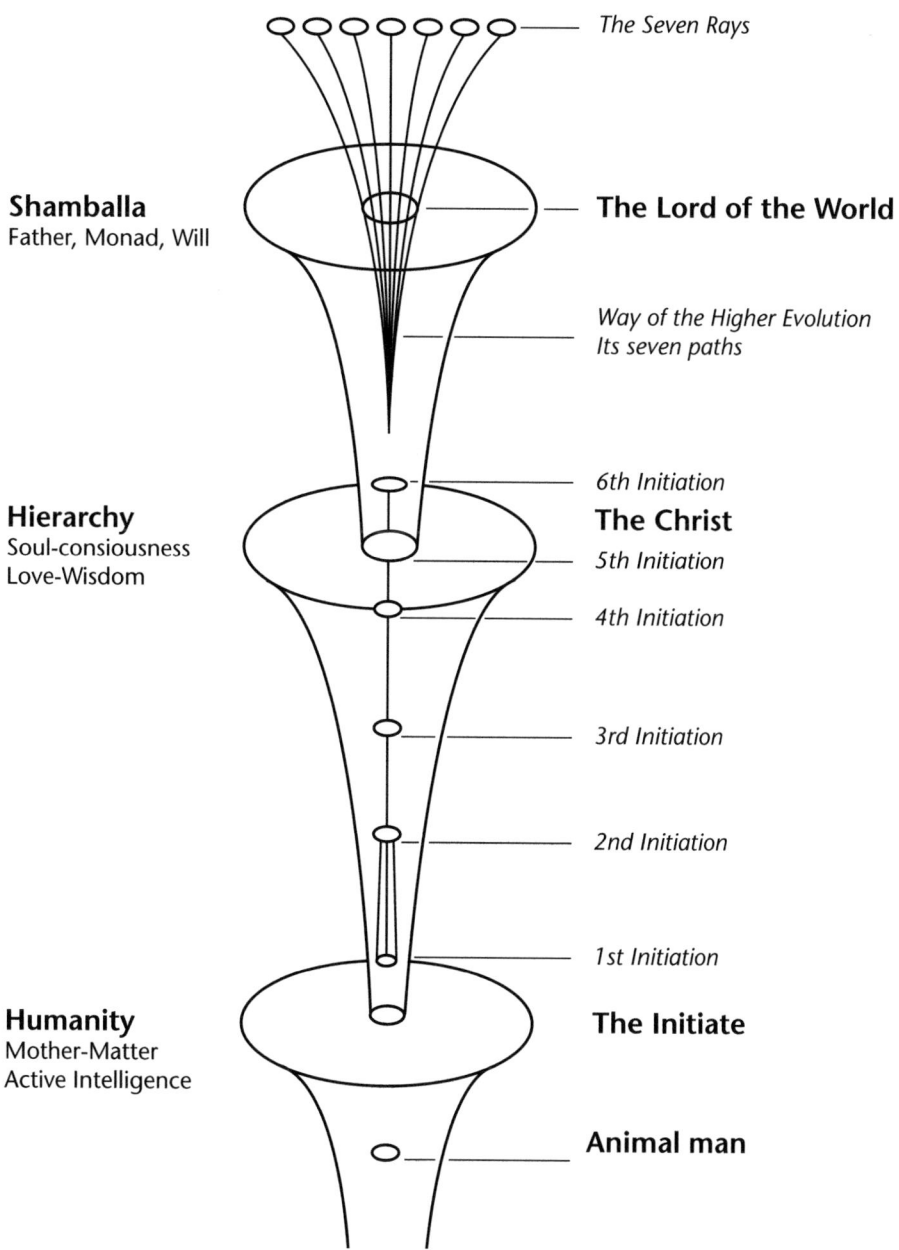

The Seven Rays

Shamballa
Father, Monad, Will

The Lord of the World

*Way of the Higher Evolution
Its seven paths*

6th Initiation
The Christ

Hierarchy
Soul-consiousness
Love-Wisdom

5th Initiation

4th Initiation

3rd Initiation

2nd Initiation

1st Initiation

Humanity
Mother-Matter
Active Intelligence

The Initiate

Animal man

*Chart 7.
The Antahkarana connects the initiate with the Hierarchy and Christ.*[33A]

Projection, has been carefully undertaken by the disciple and he has at least some measure of clear perception as to the work he has done by the dual means of spiritual living and scientific, technical, occult work. He is therefore himself invocative. His life effect is registered upon the higher levels of consciousness and he is recognised as "a point of invocative tension." This tension and this reservoir of living energy, which is the disciple himself, is set in motion by projected thought, the use of the will and a sounded Word or Phrase of Power.

The result is that his developed potency and its radius of influence are now sufficiently strong to call out a response from the Spiritual Triad. There is then a going forth towards the aspect of the antahkarana, constructed by the disciple, along which the life of soul and body can travel. The Father (Monad), working through the thread, now goes forth to meet the Son (the soul, enriched by the experience of personality life in the three worlds), and from the higher levels a line of responsive projection of energy is sent forth which will eventually make contact with the lower projection. Thus the antahkarana is built. *The tension of the lower evokes the attention of the higher.*

This is the technical process of invocation and evocation. There is a gradual approach from both the divine aspects. Little by little, the vibration of both becomes stronger reciprocally. There comes then a moment when contact between the two projections is made in meditation. This is not a contact between soul and personality (the goal of the average aspirant), but a contact between the fused soul and personality energy and the energy of the Monad, working through the Spiritual Triad. This does not constitute a moment of crisis, but is in the nature of a Flame of Light, a realisation of liberation, and a recognition of the esoteric fact that a man is himself the Way. There is no longer the sense of personality and soul or of ego and form, but simply the One, functioning on all planes as a point of spiritual energy and arriving at the one sphere of planned activity by means of the path of Light. In considering this process, words prove completely inadequate. At this stage, when very advanced, there is no form attracting the Monad outwards into manifestation. There is no way in which the call of matter or of form can evoke a response from the Monad. There remains only the great pull of the consciousness of humanity as a whole and to this, response can be made via the completed antahkarana. Down - or rather across - this bridge, descent can be made at will, in order to serve humanity and to carry out the will of Shamballa.

This is a statement of the final consummation. But before that can take place in its perfected completion, there must be a long period of gradual approach of the two aspects of the bridge - the higher, emanating from the Spiritual Triad, in response to monadic impulse, and the lower, emanating from the personality, aided by the soul - across the chasm of the separating mind. Finally, contact between that which the Monad projects and that which the disciple is projecting is made, and then come the fifth and sixth stages."[34]

Working on and understanding invocation and evocation is extremely important to the freemason. Chart 7 shows how the result i.e. evocation is evoked through persistent invocation. Thus when life is totally invocative evocation of the will takes place. Life is first and foremost invocative when a fusion of personality and soul exists, and the true operate as a consciously merged and focused entity.

Through his inner work, occult meditation, the true master builder grasps the Plan of God and manifestates it physically. The true master builder provides his inner nature to God so that His Plan can be manifestated physically, and he surrenders his inner nature to God so that the Light of God can flow through his bodies and into the lower realms of nature and into mankind. The true master builder seeks nothing for himself, but is solely focused on expressing the will of God.

The master builder works on the seventh plane, but carries out his work according to the third and the first plane. He works under guidance of the ray-lord of the seventh ray. Master Rakoczy works for freemasonry and he is now Mahachohan, and for a long period he has co-operated closely with the Master on the first ray.

The Brotherhood of Man

"Brotherhood, as it essentially is, constitutes a major mystery."
Djwahl Kuhl.

"Much has been written, preached and talked about brotherhood. So much has been said and so little brotherhood practised that the word has fallen somewhat into disrepute. Yet the word is a statement of the underlying origin and goal of humanity and is the keynote of the fourth kingdom in nature, the human.

Brotherhood is a great natural fact; all men are brothers; under the divergences of colour, creed, cultures and civilizations, there is only one humanity without distinction or differences in its essential nature, in its origin, its spiritual and mental objectives, its capacities, its qualities and its mode of development and of evolutionary unfoldment. In these divine attributes (for that is what they are) all men are equal; it is only in relation to time and in the extent to which progress has been made in the revelation of innate divinity in all its fullness that temporary differences become apparent.

In every human heart the divine is eternally present and it is the background to brotherhood." [35]

"Each form of life from Logos to the atom includes a soul-aspect and all souls are connected to the World-Soul. This is the foundation of the scientific belief in brotherhood of man. Brotherhood of man is a fact in nature – not an ideal."[36]

"It is through the realisation of that connection that the true expression of the brotherhood of man can appear. All men are sons of the Father and, therefore, brothers. All men are divine; some men are already God-conscious and expressing divinity and some are not. Some men know Christ, because the

Christ in them is active while others are entirely unaware of the divine Being hidden deep within their hearts. There is only difference in degree of consciousness; there is no difference in nature.

Men enables themselves to realise the inner brotherhood through the establishing of right human relations and the cultivation of goodwill." [37]

"Yet if men carried the concept of brotherhood with all its implications into the life and work of every day, into all intercourse whether between the capitalist and the labourer, the politician and the people, between nation and nation, or between race and race, there would emerge that peace on earth which nothing could upset or overturn. So simple a rule, and yet utterly beyond the mental grasp of the majority!"[38]

"Astral energies emanating from the new sign of the zodiac into which we are now entering, the sign Aquarius. This sign, that of the water-carrier, is a living sign and an emotional sign. It will (through the effect of its potent force) stimulate the astral bodies of men into a new coherency, into a brotherhood of humanity which will ignore all racial and national differences and will carry the life of men forward into synthesis and unity. This means a tide of unifying life of such power that one cannot now vision it, but which - in a thousand years - will have welded all mankind into a perfect brotherhood."[39]

"When we come to the consideration of other basic trends in the world of current thought it becomes apparent that one of the most dominant is the increasing emphasis laid upon group consciousness, or environal awareness. No longer does the man live in the interests of the separated self but he begins to realize the need for adjustment to and in the condition of his neighbor. He assumes the duty of being in a very real sense his brother's keeper, and realizes that in reality progress, contentment, peace of mind and prosperity do not exist for him apart from that of his brother. This realization is steadily expanding to include bigger and bigger groups and at the end the whole humanity. The necessity of giving instead of getting is growing in the racial consciousness and the recognition of certain of the basic concepts connected with brotherhood is steadily growing. Brotherhood as a fact in nature is as yet largely a theory, but brotherhood as an ideal is now fashioned in the racial consciousness."[40]

"The Kingdom of God can appear on earth, and this in the immediate future, but the members of this kingdom recognize neither rich nor poor, neither high nor low, neither labour nor capital but only the children of the one Father, and the fact - natural and yet spiritual - that all men are brothers. Here lies the solution of the problem with which we are dealing. The spiritual Hierarchy of our planet recognizes neither capital nor labour; it recognizes only men and brothers. The solution is, therefore, *education and still more education* and the adaptation of the recognized trends of the times to the vision seen by the spiritually minded and by those who love their fellowmen." [41]

One thing is what men experience about brotherhood on their own stage of development, in microcosmos. Another thing is the mystery of brotherhood itself in macrocosmos.

"Brotherhood, as it essentially is, constitutes a major mystery; also it is one which is only in process of solving, and that only on the two higher levels of the cosmic physical plane - those levels which we call the logoic and the monadic.

I am aware that you understand brotherhood in terms of the One Father and His children. That understanding is in itself so limited and inaccurate that it serves mainly to distort the truth; yet all that you can grasp at this time is embodied in this concept. The nearest description of the true relationship might be said to be as follows: Brotherhood is an expression of the relation which the planetary Logos (on the cosmic mental plane) bears to His Personality as it expresses itself through the planet with all its forms of life, upon the cosmic physical plane; this relationship is focussed through Sanat Kumara Who is the individualised Mind of that great Life. Wording it otherwise, the planetary Logos on His Own plane is to Sanat Kumara what the soul is to the human personality upon the physical plane in the three worlds. The sum total of the relation and of the relationships set up is, therefore, inadequately covered by the word "brotherhood." "Fellowship," so frequently used to express a similar idea, is in reality the mode whereby a dimly sensed brotherhood seeks to make its presence felt. The words "the fellowship of Christ" indicate the emergence of this concept subjectively upon the mental plane; this will be followed, as time elapses, by concrete manifestation upon the physical plane. It is this idea which lies behind the glibly used words "idea, ideal and idol," and which is also responsible for the growing sense of responsibility which characterises all human advancement upon the way of life. It is this basic idea which governs the Council Chamber at Shamballa and which constitutes the motivating impulse behind the planetary expression of livingness. It is this also which characterises the ideal for which the Hierarchy stands and which implements the Plan; it is this spiritual planning which results in the growing "forms of relationship" which today seem to be taking definite shape in the concretising of the divine project: Right Human Relations." [42]

"The objectives of the hierarchical work must be emphasised and the nature of the divine Plan unfolded so that purpose and goal may be presented to humanity; the synthesis of the chain of hierarchical Existences - from the smallest atom of matter up to and including the Lord of Life Himself - must be unfolded; the essential and spiritual interdependence of all and the interrelation of every unit of divine life must be proved. This will eventually lead to that established unity of effort which will express itself in the merging of the fourth and the fifth kingdoms in nature, and to the establishment of that brotherhood which will constitute the germ or the seed of the coming manifestation of *the Hierarchy as the Heart of God* (directly related to the Heart of the Sun) in physical expression."[43]

The true Brother and Sister recognize their own divinity, their own inner Christ.

The true Brother and Sister recognize their own connection with the Divine, with God and with Christ.

The true Brother and Sister recognize their unity with all other souls through the Divine.

Service

*"The building of the antahkarana is the greatest and highest service
that true aspirants can offer."*
Djwahl Kuhl

"The Law of Service has been thus outlined in an endeavor to make one of
the most esoteric influences in the solar system somewhat clearer in our minds.
I call you to service, but would remind you that the service discussed here will
only be possible when we have a clearer vision of the goal of meditation, and
learn to preserve, during the day, the attitude of inner spiritual orientation.
As we learn to obliterate and efface out of our consciousness ourselves as the
central figure in our life drama, then and then only can we measure up to our
real potentialities as servers of the Plan."[44]

Definition of service

"The definition of this word is not easy. There has been too much attempt
to define it from the angle of personality knowledge. Service can be briefly
defined as the spontaneous effect of soul contact. This contact is so definite
and fixed that the life of the soul can pour through into the instrument which
the soul must perforce use upon the physical plane. It is the manner whereby
the nature of that soul can demonstrate in the world of human affairs. Service is
not a quality or a performance; it is not an activity towards which people must
strenuously strive, nor is it a method of world salvage. This distinction must be
clearly grasped, or else our whole attitude to this momentous demonstration of
the success of the evolutionary process in humanity will be at fault.

Service is *a life demonstration*. It is *a soul urge*, and is as much an evolutionary impetus of the soul as the urge to self-preservation or to the reproduction of the species is a demonstration of the animal soul. This is a statement of importance. It is a soul instinct, if we may use such an inadequate expression and is, therefore, innate and peculiar to soul unfoldment. It is the outstanding characteristic of the soul, just as *desire is the outstanding characteristic of the lower nature*. It is group desire, just as in the lower nature it is personality desire. It is the urge to group good. It cannot, therefore, be taught or imposed upon a person as a desirable evidence of aspiration, functioning from without and based upon a theory of service. It is simply the first real effect, evidenced upon the physical plane, of the fact that the soul is beginning to express itself in outer manifestation."[45]

"They must learn to lay the emphasis upon soul contact and upon an active familiarity with the egoic life, and not upon the form side of service. May I beg those of you who respond to these ideas and are sensitive to soul impression (oft-times misinterpreting the truth, being biassed by personality ends) to lay the emphasis upon soul contact and not upon the form side of service. Activity of the form side lays stress upon personality ambition, veiling them with the glamour of service. If care over the essential of service - soul contact - is taken, then the service rendered will flow with spontaneity along the right lines and bear much fruit. Of this, the selfless service and the deep flow of spiritual life, which have been demonstrated in the world work of late, is a hopeful indication."[46]

The Law of Service is the law that has been designated to govern all soul contact.

Three things require our attention when we study this law.

"First, is the fact that *the result of all contact achieved in meditation and the measure of our success, will be determined by the ensuing service to the race.* If there is right understanding, there will necessarily be right action.

It has previously been pointed out that the three great sciences which will come to the fore in the New Age, and which will lead humanity from the unreal to the real, and from aspiration to realisation are

1. The science of Meditation, the coming science of the mind.
2. The science of Antahkarana, or the science of the bridging which must take place between higher and lower mind.
3. The science of Service, which is a definite technique of at-one-ment.

Secondly, this Law of Service is something which may not be escaped.

Thirdly this Law of Service was expressed for the first time fully by the Christ two thousand years ago. He was the forerunner of the Aquarian Age, and hence His constant emphasis upon the fact that He was the "water of life", the "living water" which men needed. Hence the esoteric name of this law is that of "water and the fishes." The Piscean age slowly, very slowly, prepared the way for the divine expression of service, which will be the glory of the coming centuries. Today, we have a world which is steadily coming to the realization that "no man liveth unto himself", and that only as the love, about which so much has been written and spoken, finds its outlet in service, can man begin to measure up to his innate capacity."[47]

The true server

"These characteristics can be easily and briefly noted. They are not exactly what one may have been led to believe. I am not here speaking of the qualifications required for the treading of the Path of Discipleship or the Probationary Path. These are well known. They are the platitudes of the spiritual life, and constitute the battleground, or the Kurukshetra of most aspirants. We are here concerned with those qualities which will emerge when a man is working under the impulse of the Law of Service. They will appear when he is a real channel for the life of the soul. His major characteristics will then be three in number:

1. He will be distinguished, as might be expected, by the quality of *harmlessness*, and by an active refraining from those acts and that speech which might hurt or cause any misunderstanding. By no word, suggestion

implication, innuendo or voiced dissatisfaction will he hurt his group. You will note that I do not say "will not hurt any individual." Those working under the Law of Service need no reminder not to hurt any individual. They often need, under the exuberance of spiritual stimulation and the intensity of their aspiration, to be reminded to demonstrate group harmlessness.

2. The second characteristic is *a willingness to let others serve as seems best to them*, knowing that the life flowing through the individual server must find its own channels and outlets, and that direction of these currents can be dangerous and prevent the rendering of the intended service. The server's efforts will be turned in two directions:

   a. To the task of helping others to "stand in spiritual being", as he himself is learning to stand.
   b. To aiding the individual to express his service in his chosen field as he desires to express it, and not as the onlooking helper deems that he should do it.

One point might here be made clear. The task of those who are working under the Law of Service is not exerted primarily with that group in the world today which is working under the effect of that general response to which we earlier referred. These effects are easily shepherded into those activities which, en masse, work out as philanthropic endeavor, as educational experiments, or social efforts in the life of the community. The name of those who thus respond is legion, and the will to serve in this particular way needs no impetus. The remarkable response to the many recent campaigns to good will definitely evidenced this. But the work of the new type of server is directed towards those who are establishing soul contact and who can therefore work under the new incoming Aquarian Law. This centres around the capacity to stand, not only in spiritual being, but together with others, *working with them subjectively, telepathically, and synthetically.*

This distinction merits attention for one can easily waste effort by entering fields already well handled from the point of view of the attainment of the units in that field.

3. The third characteristic of the new server is *joyfulness*. This takes the place of criticism (that dire creator of misery) and is *the silence that sounds*.

It would be well to ponder on these last words, for their true meaning cannot be conveyed in words, but only through a life dedicated to the newer rhythms and to the service of the whole. Then that "sounding joy" and that "joyful sounding" can make its true meaning felt."[48]

"The Master looks not at a worker's worldly force or status, not at the numbers of people who are gathered around his personality but at *the motives* which prompt his activity and at the effect of his influence upon his fellowmen.

True service is the spontaneous outflow of a loving heart and an intelligent mind.

True service is the result of being in the right place and staying there; it is produced by the inevitable inflow of spiritual force and not by strenuous physical plane activity; it is the effect of a man's being what he truly is, a divine Son of God, and not by the studied effect of his words or deeds.

A true server gathers around him those whom it is his duty to serve and aid by the force of his life and his spiritualised personality, and not by his claims or loud speaking. In self-forgetfulness he serves; in self-abnegation he walks the earth, and he gives no thought to the magnitude or the reverse of his accomplishment and has no pre-conceived ideas as to his own value or usefulness. He lives, serves, works and influences, asking nothing for the separated self."[49]

"And yet, in spite of all this which indicates wrong motives and false aspiration, service of a kind is constantly and readily being rendered. Humanity is on its way to a right understanding of services; it is becoming responsive to this new law and is learning to react to the steadily imposing will of that great Life who informs the constellation Aquarius, just as our solar Logos informs our solar system and our planetary Logos informs our earth planet.

The idea of service is, at this time, the major idea to be grasped for (in grasping it) we open ourselves wide to the new incoming influences. The Law of Service is the expression of the energy of a great Life, who, in cooperation with Him "in Whom we live and move and have our being", is subjecting the human family to certain influences and streams of energy which will eventually do three things:

1. Awaken the heart centre in all aspirants and disciples.
2. Enable emotionally polarised humanity to focus intelligently in the mind.
3. Transfer the energy of the solar plexus into the heart.

This unfolding of what we might call "the consciousness of the heart" or the development of true feeling is the first step towards group awareness. This group awareness and this identification with the feeling aspect of all groups is the quality which leads to service - a service to be rendered as the Masters render it, and as the Christ demonstrated it for us in Galilee."[50]

"The sign for the Aquarian Age is that of a man, carrying on his shoulders a jar of water so full that it pours over to all and sundry, and yet it diminishes not. The sign for this Law of Service is very similar, but the difference lies in this; that the man stands, perfectly balanced in the form of a cross, with arms stretched out and with the water pot upon his head. In this difference there lies much of real significance. The jar of water, posed upon the shoulders, is a sign of the burden of service. It is not easy to serve. Man is today only beginning to learn how to serve. The jar of water upon the head of the man, who has been upon the cross of sacrifice for so long a time that the position has become to him perfectly natural, indicates that the cross, which has upheld him for so long, has now disappeared. The man with the water jar upon his head indicates to us poise, equilibrium and balance. For this balance, the understanding of the Law of Magnetic Impulse has prepared him. That is the Law of Polar Union and its symbol is the originator of the zodiacal sign for the constellation Libra - balance and service. These are the two expressions of Divinity which are, today, man's next great objective."[51]

Restoration of Freemasonry?

"The pharisees and the scribes had received the keys of knowledge,
but they had hidden them.
They themselves did not enter,
and those who wished to enter were not allowed."
Th. Logion 39

Vision

As mentioned freemasonry has great potential to restore the mysteries in the Aquarian age. The influences from Aquarius and the seventh ray will help
- man to enter through the gateway of initiations
- man to function as an integrated personality
- man to recognize himself as a creator
- humanity to become a channel for distribution of spiritual energy
- man to recognize himself as a part of a group

Thus man is able to become *a true master builder.*

In order to arrive at the above much work has to be done.

Each individual, every freemason has to work with himself in a concrete way and not only symbolically. That implies that he must cleanse the bodies in actual fact and in actual fact integrate the personality. In addition to that he must connect to his soul through meditation and build the antahkarana. Finally he must practise service.

The freemason-lodge must do the same. It must free itself of everything belonging to the world of personality. It must be effectuated in the open lodge as well as in the fields of organization and instructions. In addition conscious work must be done to build a channel through which the Light and Power of God can flow. Finally conscious work must be done with instreaming in the lodge in order that the lodge will become a true center of instreaming where the divine life can steam into humanity and the realms of Earth.

Getting started

When a lodge, a craft or federation are preparing to change certain things in their work according to the spiritual laws, some questions need to be asked both to yourself and eachother.

A question could be: Do we really want to change anything?

Then you may ask: Do we indeed have the will to make the requisite changes? Each individual wishes to be good and noble in motives and deeds, and each indiviual wishes to do things as well as possible. And each individual does the his best! Each individual does the best from the stage where he is on the ladder of development. If you work in a lodge you have done your best based on the assumptions and understandings you have and according to the directions that you have received.

When you then become aware of the fact that the work to be done can be understood on another plane and on a completely different level, and when this understanding rings true deep in your heart, the question arises: How do I or we get there?

The greatest obstacles to seeking the new knowledge is to be found in ourselves: in our emotions, in our conceptions and thought-patterns and in old habits.

That is why you have to ask youself deep within: Do I – do we in our lodge actually wish to work to restore the mysteries? Do we in actual fact have the courage and the will to work when we will possibly loose some pleasures of the personality? Are we willing to risk changing former conceptions about ourselves and about work in the lodge? Am I willing and ready to put myself aside and instead dedicate my personality to working for the inner worlds? Am I ready to work deeply with myself and to discipline my life according to spiritual principles?

When the individual Sister or Brother wishes and seriously has the will to work, and when the lodge or the craft has the wish and will to do so, the question arises: How do we get started? A gigantic challange is ahead.

Two stages

The following may be of help getting started.

Two stages are involved in working of restoring the mysteries:

First there will be a transition-stage where the present Sisters and Brothers and those who join in along the way have to go through an education which gives the students possibility *really* to develop. The following chapter gives an example of such an education.

As knowledge, understanding and consciousness of the inner worlds grow as a result of this education the lodge has to cleanse itself for what belongs to the personality, and slowly starts to function according to the life of the soul and the spirit.

This process will probably be of long durance and has possibly to be repeated on still new levels. Each time Sisters and Brothers must cleanse themselves even more, and their consciousness will increase in line with their soul contact being established, expanded and stabilized.

The length of time nessecary for the work on this first stage naturally depends on the work that is done: the regularity, the discipline and the depth of the work.

In A.A. Baileys books D.K. says, that the rituals must be cleansed of various influences and brought into accordance with the esoteric teachings. That can first be done when a group within the lodge or the federation has reached so far in their inner development that they are able to work through occult meditation.

Next stage will come when the lodge is able to function according to its purpose and as it is predicted. Then all Sisters and Brothers will be true columns of light in the Temple of the Lord.

Teachings in mysteries
- on the pathway of restoration

As it is stressed again and again it is crucial to start educating those who seek spiritual development and who wish to be servers of the Kingdom of God here on Earth.

If lodges and crafts are to take their purpose seriously and cooperate to restore the mysteries, they have to consider the education of present new sisters and brothers and newcomers. It is possible that the way education has been practised so far has to be rejected totally, but it is also possible that parts of it may be used.

It is crucial that the focus in the education is balanced between *knowledge, wisdom and understanding,* a balance between *studies, meditation and service,* a balance between *analog and digital thinking*, between *vertical and horizontal thinking.* In addition teaching has to be progressive so that it supports each individual sister and brother in their development towards the purpose.

When you begin a more extensive piece of work you must plan profoundly. When we talk about planning in connection to work in a lodge or another esoteric group the method is primarily occult meditation on the subject to be worked on. Through meditation you can receive inspiration of the vision to which you are aspiring, and you have to work on *the intention* of the vision. When a human wishes to reach the peak of the mountain, the intention should be the star standing and shining over the peak of the mountain. So high up and so radiant the intention must stand.

To reach forth to the peak of the mountain there will be many smaller hills and many minor crests to be forced. On his journey to the peak of the mountain man sets himself many subordinated goals, and these many subordinated goals will at last bring him forth to the peak.

When you are planning a piece of work you must have the purpose in mind the whole time, and at the same time you have the next subordinated goal in mind. This will bring the student forth on his journey.

To achieve the next goal knowledge has to be acquired. There will be required meditative exercises on symbols and ideas which give subjective knowledge and experience. There will be tasks and exercises to be done in order to achieve deeper understanding of the acquired objective and subjective experiences.

The duty of the companion is to organize the path with knowledge, meditation and exercises so that the pilgrim is enabled to reach the next peak of a mountain. In ancient Greece such a companion was called a pedagogue. A pedagogue knows the path, he knows the pitfalls, mounds on the path, and he knows many divertions to reach the goal. He walks beside the disciple, but he does not walk the path for him. The pedagogue is the teacher.

The education has to be pedagogically planned, i.e. thus there is a progression in the work. Always the contents must build on previous knowledge and understandings so that the disciple has a foundation on which to acquire and understand the next step.

Inspiration to teaching

During the work to understand the core and purpose of freemasonry the author had a vision of freemasonry in the future: a Temple shone so radiantly, and the beauty, love and power of the inner worlds overflooded the Temple and columns of men and streamed into Earth and Mankind.

The Master D.K. has stated
-   that freemasonry in the new age will return to its original roots and cleanse its distortions
-   that freemasonry in the new age will not merely work on a symbolic level, but that it will work *in actual fact*, i.e. as the degrees illustrates so will it be carried out in reality
-   that freemasonry will assist God in creating the Kingdom of God on Earth

What could be done in order to reach the revealed vision? To find out the author worked meditatively on it for several years. At one point the author got an inspiration which can be seen in chart 8.

The diagram shows the purpose of education of the disciples in freemasonry, and it shows that there are three high mountain peak, namely the first, the second and the third degree.

The goals of realization express what the disciple experiences inside himself. These cannot to be measured by others; only the disciple himself *knows* if the goal of realization is about to be achieved, is achieved or unable to be experienced or realized altogether. So only the statement of the disciple can tell, however the motives and the attitudes of the disciple will reflect the truth of his words.

Goals of knowledge express the goals that the disciple has to achieve concerning the acquiring of knowledge and skills. Knowledge is achieved through studies. Skills are learned through training and practising various innate potentials. Knowledge and skills can be measured externally.

Contents express the subjects that will be relevant to work on to assist the disciple to reach his goals and also to help the disciple attain greater consciousness and increased understanding of the work he will be doing in the logde.

The underlined words point to the part of the human constitution which the concerned degree especially has to focus on. Therein you see a progression as the focus goes from personality to soul to spirit. The same is seen when you first work on concentration, then meditation and finally contemplation.

The methods used in education are prioritized, and evidently meditation-exercises are first and mental studies last. This indicates the need of emphasising teaching in meditation extremely high and supporting the disciples in a pedagogical planned meditation-practice.

Furthermore is seen, that in all three degrees work has to be done on studies, meditation and learning-by-doing, which means learning rituals, signs ect. by training and exercising in practice. Rituals and signs obviously have to be known, but *the most important is to know and understand what they mean on the inner planes*. This understanding is acquired by *making* the signs and by *meditating on signs and ritual*. Through understanding and increased consciousness the effect of the concerned sign and ritual will be strengthened when used in open lodge.

Free-

Purpose: - to become a server of God on Earth
- to transmit love, power and beauty of

	Goals of realization	Goals of knowledge
1st degree	- E.A. experiences himself united with God on a inner level - E.A. experiences himself as a cell in Gods whole creation	- E.A. has a regular practise of meditation - E.A. disciplines his day and time - E.A. has cleansed his physical, etheric, astral and mental body
2nd degree	- F.C. experiences to be able to be in contact with his soul-aspect - F.C. realizes that he is a server of God	- F.C. works consciously on to build the bridge to the soul through meditation F.C. devotes regular time to service - F.C. acquires knowledge about …. see contents
3rd degree	- M.M. is predominatly guided by impulses of the soul - M.M. knows and realizes his work of service	- M.M. extends co-operation with the soul and God - M.M. works consciously on transmitting the light and love of God - M.M. continously seeks to grasp the Plan and Will of God

mason

God to Earth and all its realms through our bodies and inner being

Contents	Methods	Timeframe
- the constitution of man - the 7 planes of existences - the three: spirit – soul – body - concentration, meditation, contemplation - the third ray - involution – evolution - development of man: personality	(in prioritized succession) - "cleansing"-exercises and analog exercises - learning by doing - studies	
- the science of the soul - the five - the science of meditation - the second ray - development of consciousness - development of man: soul	- meditation - visualization-exercises - studies - learning by doing	
- the seven - contemplation - the first ray - development of man: spirit - man and cosmos	- meditation - contemplation - studies - learning by doing	

Chart 8. Inspiration received by Else Marie Post, the 10th of Sept. 2007.

Time frame. During the inspiration the blank frame was there, but nothing came into it. In the authors own understanding it must be so because it is always important to have a time frame. Consciousness and sub-consciousness then adjust to the work which is to be done. Lack of time frame can blur the work make it go on indefinitely, and in that way it is never carried out.

As in every sequence of teaching there must be *distinctness of purpose, goals, contents and work, both in extent and time to be used.* This concerns a whole sequence e.g. the whole first degree or a entire year in the lodge, and it concerns each education lesson.

As in all spiritual work education has to take place *regularly.*

When planning work concerning the individual degree a detailed program has to be prepared containing goals, contents, set work and time to be used of each lesson.

It is the responsibility of the teacher to work out a specific plan.

Most often people with definte offices are responsible for the education. In the period of transition i.e. when a lodge moves *from symbolic work to real work* it can be necessary to deviate this principle.

Like elsewhere where education takes place the educator must himself have experience and personal knowledge of the subject being taught. If necessary an external teacher must be brought in.

The water-carrier

"Teacher, which is the most important commandment in the Law?"
Jesus answered:
"You shall love the Lord your God with all your heart,
and with all your soul, and with all your mind.
This is the first and most important of the commandments.
But after this there is another one very similar to it:
You shall love your neighbour as yourself."
Matth. 22, 37-40

The Water-carrier is a person who within has a pitcher with living water that pours out to everything and everybody. The pitcher is constantly filled up from an inner fountain and is forever full. It constantly flows over to everything and everybody who is in need of living water.

The water-carrier is the true server who has built a channel to the inner worlds, and the inner worlds can now spread out light, love and power through this channel and into the lower worlds.

"The light must enter vertically and be diffused or radiated horizontally." This creates the cross of service upon which the disciple is pendant until the Cross of Sanat Kumara is revealed to him." [52]

In the Piscean age the purpose of Christ was to connect mankind with the Hierarchy. The Hierarchy is the centre through which love and wisdom of God can stream into humanity. Humans should be encouraged to enter into communities and into being related to all people of Earth and thus unite and *share* "bread and wine" in the presence of Christ.

In the Piscean age the horizontal principle was stressed.

In the Aquarian age the vertical principle will be weighted.

In the Aquarian age the work of Christ will be to connect disciples to the higher centre from whence the Father is contacted, Shamballa. Here recognition of sonship is established and the divine purpose can be known. Man will realize his at-one-ment with Christ, and thus he will understand his connection with God. Man will develop his consciousness and realize his unity with sisters and brothers. Humanity will melt to an entity, and universalism will spread.

In the Aquarian age disciples must develop deeper subjective relations and an increased sensitivity to impressions and inspiration from higher levels. Thus *the vertical life of the spirit* will stream in, and *the horizontal life of relationship* will be expressed as true brotherhood.[53]

When Christ was here at the beginning of the Piscean age he taught us the significance of *renunciation and crucifixion.*

The astrological sign Pisces is one of the arms on the astrological movable cross, which is also referred to as the ordinary cross or the cross of the personality. It is connected to the actions of humanity. In that age man was to learn to renunciate selfish interests and personal pleasures, and instead focus on fellowman.

The water-carrier is one of the arms on the fixed cross, which is also referred to as the cross of the soul. This cross is connected to the Hierarchy. The fixed cross focuses on development of consciousness, development of the soul.

When Christ reappears and influences development in the Aquarian age, his mission will be the *resurrection.* Humans will shift their focus from being preoccupied with their personal life which might be strenuous and laborious, to being engaged with spiritual life and being of service of the Most High. The inner realization of being at-one with the divine and with all creations in nature makes the service easy and joyfull.

"*The resurrection is not the rise of the dead from their tombs but the passage from the death of self-absorption to the life of unselfish love, the transition from the darkness of selfish individualism to the light of universal spirit, from falsehood to truth, from the slavery of the world to the liberty of the eternal....*

... Creation .... groaneth and travaileth in pain .... to be delivered from the bondage of corruption into the liberty of the glory of the children of God."[54]

So resurrection can be defined thus that only that lives on which has a divine aspect and which is integrated in the entity of life and consciousness which we call God.

Just as the individual man and humanity as a whole develops under influence of the great astrological cycles, likewise the freemason-lodge is influenced.

Within the lodge the movable cross relates to the E.A.-degree, while the fixed cross relates to the F.C.-degree and the cardinal cross to the M.M.-degree.

When time now changes from the movable cross to the fixed cross, freemasonry will be helped moving the focus from the universe of the personality to the universe of the soul.

When we also are told that Christ will help us focus our attention and our work on the resurrection, it will become possible for freemasonry to realize the resurrection in reality and not just on a symbolic level.

When the freemason has finished his work on the movable cross and has moved on to the fixed cross, he also will be able to join in building a universal religion.

Religion comes from 'religare', which means 'to connect or create bonds backward', i.e. to connect or create bonds back to the fountain of creation. Religions are meant to help man to find his way back to God and help him to discover God in the outer and in the inner.

In future the term 'religion' will be used concerning the invocation of humanity and the evocation of the larger life-entity.

As the new religion will be universal there will be *one* humanity, and this humanity will become a true brotherhood regardless of nationalities, political opinions, creeds, races etc.

In the Aquarian age freemasonry will have unique and exceptional potential to develop into *a true and real* brotherhood.

Freemasonry will have unique and exceptional potential to establish schools where men can learn about the mysteries of life, and how to form themselves in the light from the Most High.

The freemason will have the possibility of becoming *a true and real* server able to transmit light, love and power of the inner worlds to the Earth and all its realms.

The freemason will have the possibility of becoming *a true and real* builder of a universal religion.

The freemason will become *a true and real water-carrier through whom the vertical life of the spirit streams, and from whom it is sent horizontally into mankind and all realms on Earth.*

Acknowledgements

With the best of my ability and with the very best intentions I have strived to grasp and understand the ideas and visions that I have been given. With deep gratitude and great joy I have attempted to pass on in accordance with the intention behind. The ideas and visions are so extensive and so magnificent that it can be hard to encompass in a ordinary human brain and heart. If there are unclear passages or imperfect understandings it can alone be attributed to the insufficiency of my ability to receive.

To the best of my ability I have strived to pass on these ideas.

It is now up to the individual student to absorbe himself deeper and investigate the truth of the many statements.

Thank you to Esoterisk Forlag and to Kenneth Sørensen for permission to use illustrations and quotations.

A deep thanks to Annette for her persistent and affectionate support in translating this book without which this edition never would have been a reality.

Finally a deep thanks to my husbond and two sons for your love and your infinite trust, which has helped me accomplish this work.

References

Bailey, A.A.: *A Treatise on Cosmic Fire*, Lucis Press Ltd.

Bailey, A.A.: *A Treatise on White Magic*, Lucis Press Ltd.

Bailey, A.A.: *Discipleship in the New Age – Volume I*, Lucis Press Ltd.

Bailey, A.A.: *Discipleship in the New Age – Volume II*, Lucis Press Ltd.

Bailey, A.A.: *Education in the New Age*, Lucis Press Ltd.

Bailey, A.A.: *Esoteric Astrology*, Lucis Press Ltd.

Bailey, A.A.: *Esoteric Psychology - Volume I*, Lucis Press Ltd.

Bailey, A.A.: *Esoteric Psychology - Volume II*, Lucis Press Ltd.

Bailey, A.A.: *From Bethlehem to Calvary*, Lucis Press Ltd.

Bailey, A.A.: *Glamour: A World Problem*, Lucis Press Ltd.

Bailey, A.A.: *Initiation, Human and Solar*, Lucis Press Ltd.

Bailey, A.A.: *Letters on Occult Meditation*, Lucis Press Ltd.

Bailey, A.A.: *Problems of Humanity*, Lucis Press Ltd.

Bailey, A.A.: *Serving Humanity*, Lucis Press Ltd.

Bailey, A.A.: *The Destiny of the Nations*, Lucis Press Ltd.

Bailey, A.A.: *The Rays and the Initiations*, Lucis Press Ltd.

Bailey, A.A.: *The Reapperance of the Christ*, Lucis Press Ltd.

Bailey, A.A.: *The Seven Rays of Life*, Lucis Press Ltd.

Bailey, A.A.: *The Seventh Ray: Revealer of the New Age*, Lucis Press Ltd.

Besant, A.: *Esoteric Christianity*

Brøndsted, N.: *Livets indre dimension 1*, Soul Publishing (Only in Danish)

Hauge, S.: *Levende Visdom*, Lemuel Books (Only in Danish)

Hodson, G.: *Man's Supersensory and Spiritual Powers*, The Theosofiphical Publishing House

Hodson, G.: *The Call to the Heights*, The Theosofiphical Publishing House

Leadbeater, C.W.: *The Hidden Life in Freemasonry*, TPH
Leadbeater, C.W.: *Glimpses into Masonic History – Ancient Mystic Rites*, TPH
Lorentsen, A.: *Menneskets indre Univers*, Borgen (Only in Danish)
Post, E.M.: *Guddommelig rejse med Klara*, BoD (Only in Danish)
Sørensen, K.: *Fuldmånemeditation*, Virgo Publishing (Only in Danish)
World Goodwill Danmark: *Shamballa, hvor Guds vilje er kendt* (Only in Danish)

www.mysterieskole.dk

Notes

1. Reference to *Esoteric Psychology II* 345, *Esoteric Psychology I* 83-87,
   The Reapperance of the Christ 121-131, *Letters on Occult Meditation* 299-301
2. Reference to *The Rays and the Initiations* 413-419
3. Chart from *Fuldmånemeditation* 59, with permission from K. Sørensen
4. References to *Discipleship in the New Age II* 220, *Shamballa* 30,
   Fuldmånemeditation 170, *Det indre menneske* 95
5. Quotation from *The Rays and the Initiations* 330-332
6. Quotation from *Esoteric Astrology* 64
7. Quotation from *Esoteric Astrology* 444-446, *The Seventh Ray: Revealer of the New Age* 98
8. Quotation from *Esoteric Psychology I* 157, *The Seventh Ray: Revealer of the New Age* 13
9. Quotation from *Esoteric Psychology I* 59, *The Seventh Ray: Revealer of the New Age* 13-14
10. Chart from *A Treatise on Cosmic Fire* 1238, with permission from Esoterisk Center Forlag
    Reference to *Fuldmånemeditation* 90-91, *Levende Visdom* 450,
    Livets indre Dimension I 526
11. Reference to *Letters on Occult Meditation* 0, *Livets indre Dimension I* 81,
    Levende Visdom 140
12. Reference to *Esoteric Psychology I* 359 -362, *The Seventh Ray: Revealer of the New Age* 32
13. Quotation from *The Rays and the Initiations* 567,
    The Seventh Ray: Revealer of the New Age 145
14. Quotation from *Esoteric Psychology II* 345, *The Seventh Ray: Revealer of the New Age* 110
15. Quotation from *Esoteric Psychology I* 83, *The Seventh Ray: Revealer of the New Age* 25-26
16. Quotation from *The Destiny of the Nations* 107,
    The Seventh Ray: Revealer of the New Age 10
17. Quotation from *The Rays and the Initiations* 111
18. Quotation from *The Rays and the Initiations* 573-574,
    The Seventh Ray: Revealer of the New Age 148-148
19. Quotation from *The Reapperance of the Christ* 121- 131
20. Quotation from *Letters on Occult Meditation* 299-301
    The Seventh Ray: Revealer of the New Age 137-138
21. Quotation from *Letters on Occult Meditation* 303- 304
22. Reference to *Letters on Occult Meditation* 296-325

23. Reference to *A Treatise on Cosmic Fire* 569

24. Quotation from *Esoteric Psychology II* 152-153

25. Reference to *Esoteric Psychology II* 118

26. Reference to *The Rays and the Initiations* 302, *Glamour: A World Problem* 6-14.

27. Quotation from *The Rays and the Initiations* 302

28. Quotation from *Initiation, Human and Solar* 10-12

29. Quotation from *Esoteric Psychology I* 83- 85, *The Seventh Ray: Revealer of the New Age* 23

30. Quotation from *Esoteric Psychology I* 87, *The Seventh Ray: Revealer of the New Age* 24

31. Quotation from *Esoteric Astrology* 589, *The Seventh Ray: Revealer of the New Age* 19

32. Quotation from *Esoteric Psychology I* 82, *The Seventh Ray: Revealer of the New Age* 25

33. Quotation from *Discipleship in the New Age II* 429

33A.Chart from *The Rays and the Initiations* 525, with permission from Esoterisk Center Forlag

34. Quotation from *The Rays and the Initiations* 493-495

35. Quotation from *Problems of Humanity* 147-148

36. Quotation from *A Treatise on Cosmic Fire* 7

37. Reference to *Problems of Humanity* 148, 166

38. Quotation from *A Treatise on White Magic* 304, *Serving Humanity* 92

39. Quotation from *A Treatise on White Magic* 313, *Serving Humanity* 92

40. Quotation from *A Treatise on White Magic* 338-339, *Serving Humanity* 93

41. Quotation from *Problems of Humanity* 83

42. Quotation from *The Rays and the Initiations* 276

43. Quotation from *The Rays and the Initiations* 133

44. Quotation from *Esoteric Psychology II* 146

45. Quotation from *Esoteric Psychology II* 124

46. Quotation from *Esoteric Psychology II* 125

47. Quotation from *Esoteric Psychology II* 118-120

48. Quotation from *Esoteric Psychology II* 131 -133

49. Quotation from *A Treatise on White Magic* 188-189

50. Quotation from *Esoteric Psychology II* 122

51. Quotation from *Esoteric Psychology II* 122

52. Quotation from *The Rays and the Initiations* 542

53. Reference to *The Reapperance of the Christ* 79-86, *The Rays and the Initiations* 287, 542

54. Quotation from *From Bethlehem to Calvary* 260